Just Tl

To Andre

Just The Tips

365 Sales And Life Hacks To Get You Through Your Year

Just The Tips

I have to give credit for the inspiration to write this book to my amazing wife, Liz, and our incredible kids. Without them, none of this is even on my radar. And thank you to my amazing team at The CORE Finance Group for always making sure everything was getting done and for putting pressure on me to get this book finished. And a final shout out to all the MFBA LOs for the continued support and inspiration in my mortgage business, and for some great ideas for both that and this book. Thank you all.

Just The Tips

Forewords

Just The Tips

A few years ago I was introduced to small "off the strip" event held in Old Vegas at the Golden Nugget. A laid back (and somewhat obnoxious) group of loan officers were gathering for a mini-conference called #justthetip. Excuse me? And who came up with this name, and then had the audacity to have t-shirts made with that hashtag right there, *big and huge*, for all to see? Who were these people?! Could I really do this? After all I have a brand and image to uphold.

So, here I was, at this event, when this seemingly unobtrusive, casual, bearded man walks up to the front of the room wearing jeans and sneakers. Are you serious? THIS guy is sharing something about being successful? No way. He can't be a top producer. Or can he? Well, if he wasn't, I was definitely going to talk to him joining my coaching program that was for sure.

Needless to say, I was blown away. Adam Smith is a force to be reckoned with. His production levels aren't just TOP, they are through the roof. Where did he come from? Where has he been hiding? One well known fact in lending is that top producers hang together, mastermind together and share ideas. But I had never heard of Adam, and I wanted to learn more.

Just The Tips

My first action step was to introduce myself, and then I invited him as a guest on my podcast so that he could share with my listeners all about how he achieved his great success. Truth? I wanted to know for myself and interviewing him would give me the opportunity to ask the burning questions I wanted the answers to. It worked. His work style is simple and easy, it's actually amazing and I realized we all make it way too complicated.

Yet, this man hasn't fooled me. He wants you to think that he's tough, to the point, and brash, but underneath he is the biggest teddy bear, with a huge heart, extremely disciplined and knows what he wants. In the 35 years that I was a mortgage lender, I have never truly seen somebody talk the talk, and walk the walk, when it comes to nurturing his database community. Adam has this mastered and now he is sharing his #JustTheTips with you. You will soon realize the gift you are holding in your hands right now.

What a privilege and honor to be asked to write the forward to this book, and specifically for this caring man. As a coach to successful entrepreneurs, Realtors™, and loan officers struggling to break through and up the level of their practices by focusing on the gap from here to there, I'm compelled to give you a challenge.

Just The Tips

Don't just read these tips. Choose three tips you can implement today then go implement them. Maybe it's a new email signature or simply turning on the Facebook birthday calendar so you get notifications daily. Or, you could pick up your phone (because it's right next to you, anyway) and do a quick video to say "Happy Birthday" from the heart, to a client or referral partner. Watch what happens... it's called *business* silly!

Adam says these ideas aren't necessarily new or ground breaking, but some are and if you want to know what "magic pills" Adam has taken to become one of the nation's elite mega producers in the lending space (by the way, he will tell you there is no magic pill for success), then show up and do the work. Each of these tips IS a magic pill, and when consumed, they will create a heathier business.

So I ask, what are you really waiting for? A better market? The sun to shine? Interest rates to go back to 3.25%? There is absolutely no reason why even one small implemented tip won't move the needle in your practice immediately.

Adam, we thank you for this wonderful gift of you!

Jen Du Plessis, Author, Speaker, Coach, Podcast Host

Just The Tips

You know the world is getting smaller and more connected when one of your closest friendships is with someone who you have only met in person a few times, and has always lived across the country. While he has been an amazing influence in my life, my first interactions with Adam came down to a singular thought, "either this guys is a total smartass, or a complete genius." I very quickly realized the answer was a resounding yes!

I have personally been in the mortgage industry 18 years, and at the top of my company for the last several. I only say that to demonstrate I know what it takes to get to the top, and yet Adam makes it look easy. Anyone who has seen any of his numbers, his awards, his accolades, can't help but be impressed. However as you will learn reading ahead it may very well be simple enough for you to implement his advice, it is definitely not easy. There are no shortcuts to greatness, and it will take planning and grinding with a purpose to see amazing results. We are surrounded by coaches, LOs and industry professionals who make their entire way of life by selling the sizzle, while I can attest that Adam is one of the few individuals who is all steak.

This book contains more than just nice tips and false motivation. This is a real road map to actual results that put closings on the board, not just useless leads in the hopper.

On the personal side, Adam Smith is a pillar of the community, a friend, father, husband, and someone that I can truly say I look up to. The only thing bigger than this man's pipeline is his heart. If you can commit to and follow even just a small percentage of his teachings, you will level up immediately. Adam, I think I can speak for all of us when I say we cannot thank you enough for taking time out of your busy life to put this together for us all. Keep up the great work my friend.

Steve Green, Top Producing Mortgage Professional

Just The Tips

Introduction

Just The Tips

What you're going to find in the following pages is not some kind of new "fandango rocket science" marketing material. It's not bells and whistles that are going to increase your business overnight. It's not a get rich quick scheme, story or method. I'm not showing you anything revolutionary here. These are simply a year's worth of fun and random ways to essentially stay in front of clients, leads and advocates. Maybe even family and friends, too. Although, a lot of that intertwines, doesn't it? It should.

What I am giving you are 365 reminders of things you probably already know and should be implementing, or had been implementing, and quit doing for one reason or another. But you know this stuff. You just need to be reminded of it. Hopefully this will give you some good ideas to help you get closer to a strict repeat and referral business.

Sometimes we all need a reminder. Or a swift kick in the ass. Either way, this is supposed to be it. Oh, and you might find a few decent life hacks sprinkled in along the way. Particularly some travel hacks. I do quite a bit of traveling and have picked up a few ideas along the way on that subject, too.

Just The Tips

The Tips

Sales Is A Career, Not A Job

It's a marathon, not a sprint. There are no magic tricks. There is nothing that is going to make you a success overnight. A sales career takes years, or even decades, to develop so keep on keeping on.

Just The Tips

Sales Is Knowing That You Have Several Jobs

Salespeople have to know their product. Car salespeople have to know about all the different cars. Real estate agents have to know all kinds of things about neighborhoods, contracts, negotiating inspections, etc. Mortgage originators have to know different programs, rates, terms, credit and so on. And we all need to know how to generate business. It's at least two jobs.

Just The Tips

Schedule Texts To People On Their Birthdays

I use an app called Mighty Text that integrates my phone and computer and it enables me to schedule text messages for the future. It's a great tool and I can set it up to text a group of people, individually with a birthday tidings and whatever else I want like a signature that includes my www.awesomemortgageguy.com URL.

Just The Tips

Capture Birthdays From Facebook

Facebook basically gives you every single person's birthday. Put that shit in your calendar. Repeat yearly in your calendar with a couple of clicks. Now you know that person's birthday every year and can reach out to them to stay top of mind every single year. This one gets a lot of traction, I assure you.

Write

Writing, like this book for example, is a great way to gain an audience and build credibility. Write a book. Write articles for trade industry publications. Write for your local paper. Whatever. Just write. Most publications are always looking for contributors so figure out what you know about, write about it, and submit it to the publications where the audience aligns with what you know.

Just The Tips

Call People In The Morning

I do a lot of "prospecting" on the phone and I have always found that I like calling people in the morning. They haven't really gotten their day rolling yet and are usually still in a good mood before their day has beaten the crap out of them. It's a great way to start my day and motivates me for the whole day.

Call Everyone

Nobody really escapes by database and my morning calls. Clients, leads, advocates, friends, relatives, the works. Everybody either needs what you sell, knows somebody who does, or knows somebody who knows somebody who does. That person you think shouldn't be in your database because they will never need to buy from you may very well be the one person who knows a dozen others that will. Don't discount the power of those connections.

Just The Tips

Yes, Even Family

I have a dotty old great aunt in Miami Beach who is never going to use me for a mortgage. In fact, she's never going to get another mortgage. But she is still in my contact system, same as everyone else, and every time I call it's the same thing. "You're so sweet. You're such a good boy. Your father never calls. Your sister never calls." So, I get to be the favorite relative.

Don't Pay Attention To Negative News

It's just that. Negative. You need to be a positive driving force in your business and you need to make your own news. Don't like the news about the economy? Great. Go make your own economy. Upset about something our business and political leaders are doing? Fine. Go be a leader and do it the way you want.

Do Charity Work

Doing charity work is always a good thing for the community and for all mankind but volunteering with an organization you want to support will lead to meeting new people (we call these contacts), building relationships with them and eventually making clients. The neat thing about volunteering for a charity you want to support is that you're meeting people with that same interest. Instant rapport. This is a great way to add to your sphere.

Volunteer Somewhere

This is an amazing way to give back to your community, your business, your country, whatever. It will also enable you to meet new people that you have something in common with. I have volunteered or am volunteering with the Department of Defense, my local law enforcement organization, trade organizations, religious organizations and dozens of others over the years and will continue to do so, probably forever.

Just The Tips

Add Everyone To Your Database

Especially if you're new to sales. Get a database started and add everyone you know and everyone you meet to it. You can always refine it along the way but having a robust database or audience is essential to any good sales and marketing tactics and techniques that you may implement down the road.

Just The Tips

Start Working On Your Database Now

No matter what you do or how you do it, your database is the backbone. You want to do social media marketing? You need a database. You want to run an email campaign? Gotta have a database. You want to do contact management. You need a contact database. So build that sucker up. He who has the most friends, wins.

Your Email Signature File

This is a great way to make sure you are letting people know whatever you want them to know about you. The obvious contact information is important, especially in the mobile world, but it's a great way to be fun and creative about letting every single person who gets an email from you know what you want them to know about you. What you're into. What your accolades are. Whatever you want, really. It's like a mini-bio that goes out with every, single email.

Just The Tips

Congratulate People On LinkedIn

LinkedIn lets you know when your connections are celebrating birthdays, work anniversaries, promotions, job changes, publications and so on. Recognize. It's a nice thing to do and it never hurts to be top of mind with everyone all the time.

Just The Tips

Your Facebook Contact Information

This one drives me up a wall. If I had a dollar for every sales person who didn't have their contact information readily available on Facebook…well, just don't be that guy. If you're in sales, do not hide. Make it easy for people to find you for crying out loud. Are you dodging creditors or what?

Just The Tips

Post Whip Questions

Post questions on social media than enable your audience to participate and interact. People love to talk (type) about themselves and give their opinion, so let them. Questions that require an A versus B opinion are great, too. This kind of traffic boosts the visibility of your posts and spurs more comments, thereby increasing your edge rank.

Just The Tips

Socks Make Great Napkins

And if you're really, really messy like I am. I am the guy who exudes "can you bring some extra napkins", then not only do my socks make for a great napkin when no napkin is to be found, but your pant leg will then cover up the really big mess, anyway.

Just The Tips

Get Your Phone Synced With Your Computer

I know this seems remedial but seriously. You wouldn't believe how many people I come across that don't have the same data on their phones, tablets and computer. Want to make your life easier? Do this.

Just The Tips

Use The Same OS

Don't be the guy wearing an Apple watch, using a Samsung phone and carrying a Windows laptop. Get your operating systems in sync so your devices can talk to each other.

Just The Tips

Run The Same Apps Across All Your Devices

There are a thousand examples here but I use Lookout so I can log on to a computer and see where I left my phone. Or Facebook, LinkedIn, Word, Excel, and Power Point. Or ESPN, Instagram, Google, email, or Pandora. You get the idea. Your login data will match. Your preferences will match. No brainer.

Just The Tips

Get Your LinkedIn Profile Up To Snuff

LinkedIn is basically your modern day resume. And because they're in bed with Google, it's going to rank high on a Google search. If someone gives out my name, it will be Googled, I'm sure. And my LinkedIn profile will be found and people have actually contacted me and done business with me because of it.

Delete Old Apps

You know you have apps on your phone that you're not using. We all do. Those are likely either adding to draining your battery, impacting the processor speed or some other detriment to your phone. So, go and delete the ones you're not using anymore.

Just The Tips

Use Mighty Text Or Something Like It

Texting is huge now, especially with younger clients and customers. Mighty Text and its brethren make is simple to use texting, from your computer, just like you would any other electronic messaging inbox. It makes it so I don't have to look at my cell phone during the day, which I happen to really suck at.

Post On Other People's Facebook Pages

You know how Facebook works. You go to find someone, and they know someone you know. Then they know someone who's really hot. Then that person works for some cool company and all of the sudden you're eight degrees from what you started looking for. Well, we're all like that so if someone you know knows someone you want to know, this is a way that person might see you.

Just The Tips

Retweet Things From Those With A Big Audience

Want to get more Twitter followers? Then retweet things from people that have a ton of Twitter followers. This isn't much different than any other social media audience game whether it's Facebook or Instagram. You gotta give traction to get traction.

Just The Tips

Bathroom Work

This one has always cracked me up and gotten chuckles in my classes. We all do it. And you know you do it, too. I'm fortunate there's no power outlet in my water closet or I'd have hemorrhoids the size of small cars. I do some work in the bathroom first thing in the morning and I am not the only one. This window is opportune for social media posts, responding to emails, checking your calendar, etc. We're all on the can, on our phones, in the morning. Just admit it and use the time wisely instead of looking at videos of kittens.

Just The Tips

Take Good Notes

Notes are really a thing of the past except when doing meetings, conferences, etc. It's not always something you can audio or video record. Nonetheless, I use my tablet or phone and take notes if I can't record because I know I am not going to remember any of it and that I will likely want or need that data down the road.

Buy The Aisle And The Window

If you're traveling as a couple, buy the window seat and the aisle seat, rather than two seats next to each other. Odds are good that the flight won't be 100% full and the two of you might end up with your own row. Worst case, you offer the third wheel the aisle or window and sit together, anyway.

Just The Tips

Ask Everyone To Be Your Friend

You have got to stop looking at Facebook like it's strictly friends and family. It's more than just that. It's an audience. And just like someone running a TV ad from yesteryear, the more people that see it, the better the results. So, all those "friend suggestions" that Facebook makes for you…take their advice on that and friend everyone.

Just The Tips

Use The Facebook Calendar

Facebook has a great calendar. In fact, it even has EVERYONE'S birthdays on it. So, if you're using the Facebook mobile app and you're smart enough to work your smart phone calendar, everyone's birthdays are already in there. That makes it SO easy to reach out to people on their birthdays, stay top of mind again, and birthday traction is good traction.

Just The Tips

Note The Birthdays From All Your Social Media

Birthdays are a great way to stay in touch, to let people know you are thinking about them, and to let them know you care. You only have to add it to your calendar one time, repeat annually, and it's in there for life. Either their life, or yours, anyway. Again, the traction you can get from reaching out to people on their birthdays cannot be topped.

Facebook Is A Database

Most social media platforms are basically search engines. You can find almost anything, anyone or any topic with the proper search tools. Facebook, for example lets you search email addresses and phone numbers to find the people they belong to. It's a great way to connect with people when you've been given limited contact information.

Just The Tips

Mass Text People Individually

Most phones and other texting platforms will let you text multiple people without that horrible group text crap. Man, I hate getting caught up in a group text. I use Mighty Text, as I've likely already mentioned, and I can enter countless numbers into the same text and have them all sent individually so as not create that monster.

Do A Video Blog

I cannot emphasize the importance of video. For a thousand reasons, do video. From our short attention spans, to letting people know what you look like, how you speak, your wardrobe and on and on video is the most productive way to let people know who you are and what you do. Don't make excuses like you don't like how you look and sound on camera. That's how you sound and look so just do this.

Just The Tips

Ask For Zillow Reviews

If you're in real estate or mortgages, this one is crucial. Now, I am not suggesting you get into bed with Zillow. I don't like that idea and most of what is in this book is based on "no cost" ideas for selling and prospecting but Zillow is out there. And consumers use it like its freakin' Google. In fact, a lot of them start the home buying or home refinancing process there so make sure your data is up to date and that you have reviews in there. Lots of them.

Just The Tips

Ask For LinkedIn Reviews

LinkedIn is in bed with Google. Who isn't at this point? Other than Mark Zuckerberg, mind you. But if you have a robust LinkedIn profile, people are going to find it when they Google you. So, make sure you have LinkedIn reviews. I'm not talking about the clicky-clicky endorsements. I mean actual reviews. LinkedIn even makes it easy for you to ask for them. Having trouble getting people to write them? Write one for someone and it will almost be impossible from them to not reciprocate.

Just The Tips

Write LinkedIn Reviews

Writing a LinkedIn review for someone almost obligates them to write one for you. LinkedIn makes this process super easy so if you want reviews, write reviews. This is something you and your close colleagues and referral partners should be doing for each other, anyway.

Have A Short Memory

This is one of the most important skills in everything we do. I rival it to professional athletes needing this mind set. You just gave up a home run? Tough. There's another batter waiting. You just threw a pick six? Get over it. You need to be back on the field in a few minutes. You just let a goal in the five hole? It happens. The puck drops again after the commercial break. Have a short memory and move ahead to the things you do want to remember.

Endorse Someone

The "endorsement" process on LinkedIn is so easy, my toddler could do it, so why aren't you? Not only is this a great way to help out colleagues, clients, referral partners, etc. but it's also a great TOM trick. Everyone you endorse will see that you did it and it will just be another reminder that you are still out there, still doing your job.

Just The Tips

Sly Dial To Save Time

If you don't know about Sly Dial, you are going to love me for turning you on to it. You can drop a voice message straight into their voice mail box without the phone ever ringing. That's right. So, if you have a client that needs some information but once she gets it is going to rope you into a 30 minute conversation about her cats, Sly Dial is for you.

Sly Broadcast Birthday Messages

If you don't know about Sly Broadcast and the thousands of creative things you could do with it, you're missing out. I literally record a single message, like birthday tidings, and can send it out for pennies to as many people as I want. We use it for several different purposes, some others I mention in other places in this book.

Just The Tips

Maintain Your Database

Do some database maintenance and make sure people you want to contact are still in your system and review it from time to time. Past clients, advocates, referral partners, etc. Pay extra attention to those who refer you more business or use you more than once. Your database is like your car. In order to run well, it needs some periodic maintenance.

Just The Tips

Know When To Cut A Man Loose

This happens in life, and in business, and especially in sales. Is it a client that's abusive? A referral partner making your like more difficult? An employee that isn't quite getting it? Cut 'em loose. You'll be more productive in the long run and it feels oh so good.

Just The Tips

Be Social With Your Clients, Leads And Advocates

I'm not just talking about social media here. My entire social life circumnavigates around my work life. I don't do any social activities that don't involve a client, a colleague, a referral partner, and so on. We make friends before we make clients, so that's organic for us. Camping trip, clients are there. Sporting event, I brought a lead with me. Dinner at a friend's house, I likely refinanced that home.

Have Casual Conversations

My work is generally a snooze to the average person. Mortgages are boring. Nobody wants a mortgage. They want a home. Or they want to save money. Or they want to pay off debt. Or buy a new car. Or send their kid to school. The mortgage just drives that, but it's boring. When I talk to people, I want to talk about things that don't bore them. And I don't make calls to make sales. I make calls to make friends. The sales are a byproduct of that.

Just The Tips

Return Your Calls

All of them. Even the telemarketers. You never know who is at the other end of that line. I once had a guy selling branded novelty crap call me and drop a ton of names of big real estate producers in my area. We got to chatting since I know and work with a lot of these people. I never bought a single pen but I did refinance his house.

Just The Tips

You're Not The Only Car On The Road

This is the probably the only big issue I see out on the roads from day to day. Every driver seems to think they are the only driver on the road. We have very little awareness of every other car in front of us, next to us, behind us, etc. Try to focus on all the other drivers and see what it does for your road awareness.

Always Leave A Message

Unless you're just dialing the phone and letting it ring for fun, you'd better leave a message if you want a return call. Now, I know people suck at returning phone calls but do it anyway. The people you want to work with will take into consideration that you took the time to leave them a message and that it dictates the courtesy of a return phone call. Usually. Well, sometimes.

Just The Tips

Have A Fun Voice Mail Greeting

I get at least a few messages a week where people are commenting on how funny my voice mail is. And, I think it gets more people to leave messages rather than hanging up and maybe, hopefully calling back, if you're lucky. I assure you I get a better ROI on my voice mail than the boring old "I am either on the phone or away from my desk" crap most people have in their greetings.

Just The Tips

Leave Fun Messages

Voice mail messages are boring. Make your voice
mail messages fun, interesting, quirky, funny,
whatever. Voice mail has been around forever and
has been done to death. Make your messages
something people want to listen to. It will also help
get them to call you back.

Just The Tips

Capture Wedding Anniversaries

Everyone reaches out on people's birthdays, or at least they should be. Try to ramp that up by doing wedding anniversaries. Be careful, though. More than half the population gets divorced so they may not be married next year, or the year after. You don't want to wish a bitter divorcee a happy anniversary, you know?

Capture Kids Birthdays

Everyone likes to be the center of attention on their birthday, but if you're a parent, or even know a parent, you know how we beam about our kids and want THEM to be the center of attention on their birthdays. Every time you see that someone is boasting about their child's birthday, that's what I'm talking about. So note those birthdays and wish people's kids a HBD. You want people to know you're thinking about them? Let them know you're thinking about their kids.

Just The Tips

Script An Answer For What You Do

You know what your elevator speech is, so use it.
Fine tune it. Refine it. By nature, we all ask people
what they do when we first meet, so have a response
to that question that will either spark more questions,
or engage conversations. You need to be letting
people know who you are and what you do, and this
is a tried and true one to do it with.

Script An Answer For How Work Is Going

Same thing here. By nature, we ask the people we already know, those who know what we do, how work is going, so have a response to this question teed up. Make it something that is going to spawn more conversation. I always liked the response about how I had set a certain goal for myself this year, and I may fall short, so do they know anyone who might need to buy or refinance a home this year? That one's always been great for generating new contacts and leads.

Just The Tips

Learn Keyboard Shortcuts

Lifesaving stuff. For starters, I am left handed, so the mouse isn't always best for me but I know shortcuts like Alt-Tab and Ctrl-1 that are lifesavers. And I am not just talking about Windows shortcuts. They are in all the applications, too. Ctrl-P to print. Copying and pasting. Oh, boy. I probably save a quarter hour a day by using the keyboard shortcuts instead of the mouse on a ton of commands. Trust me on this one.

Just The Tips

Use Templates For Emailing And Texting

This should seem like a no-brainer but if you are sending the same emails or texts, repeatedly, then for the love of Pete create a template one time and learn how to use it over and over again. Talk about time saving stuff. We do this for dozens of different items from birthday greetings to hard core mortgage document requests.

Hotel Reward Programs

Even if you're not a regular traveler, sign up for these with every major chain. They don't cost a dime to sign up and worst case, you'll get free bottles of water and Wi-Fi when you check in.

Just The Tips

Use Your Phone To Scan Documents To PDF

Get a PDF scanner app for your phone. Documentation is all done via PDF today and when you have a hard document, or a piece of identification, or almost anything at all, you can take a picture, convert it to a PDF and now it's a small and easy way to send document. Stop sending pictures of documents. Ugh.

Just The Tips

Use 411 To Find Contact Information

Did you know there are about a thousand web resources to find contract information on potential clients? I like 411.com because of its integration with Outlook but if you really use the innerwebs properly, you can pretty much find out anything about anyone, especially how to reach them.

Use NetROnline

Did you know there's a hub of all the public records in the country? Real estate recordings, criminal records, divorces, everything. NetROnline.com is kind of a home page for all those records and narrows it down by record type, state, and county to make is easy to find what you're looking for. This one is gold in my business. I especially like when someone tells me they decided not to buy a house and the public records show they did. Good stuff.

Use PACER

If you're in an industry like mine where you need court records, learn to use PACER. That stands for Public Access to Court Electronic Records. In the mortgage business we constantly need divorce records or bankruptcy records and this is a great way to obtain what you need without making other people jump through hoops to get them. Try to minimize your clients' and customers' brain damage, you know?

Just The Tips

Either Everyone Is Your Friend Or No One Is

You can either walk through life like everyone is your friend, or like no one is. I prefer the former. Yes, I assume everyone is nice and kind and I do get burned from time to time but the latter seems horrible to me. Walking around like nobody is your friend, with that kind of paranoia and always looking over your shoulder, seems like a horrible way to live. But, I guess you never get hurt that way.
Still…

When You're Done With A Call, Set Up The Next One

No matter what your contact management system is, do not let people fall through the cracks. You just got done with a meeting? Schedule the next one. You just hung up the phone? Set up the follow up call. I have a great colleague that I sit and mastermind with every month at a local Starbucks and we don't part ways until we set up the next time we're getting together.

Just The Tips

Email To Stay TOM

Email is still an amazing tool, albeit a dying technology. It has definitely peaked. We actually use a service, that's dirt cheap, to send out an email to our entire database, twice a month with some content that the service writes, posts to our website blog and drives traffic there. It's great stuff and generates leads every time it goes out. Don't underestimate the email.

Just The Tips

No Religion, Politics or Foul Language

Seriously. This seems obvious to me but I still see a ton of sales people doing this. If you feel a need to post, or discuss, politics or religion on social media, you have too much time on your hands and need to get back to work. Go sell something. And don't use foul language in public social media venues. If you can't get your point across, in words, without swearing, you need to go back to Composition 101 or ask your school for your money back.

Search Missed Call Numbers

The internet is a great database that way. Yes, you can search on phone numbers. If that caller ID just says "wireless caller", you can do a search on it and see who the hell is calling you and not leaving messages. It might be that client or referral partner you've been trying to land. You never know.

Just The Tips

Video Helps You Make A Bond

This is huge. I cannot tell you the number of people I meet that think they already know me. They know what I look like. How I dress. What I drive. What my office looks like. How I speak. My sense of humor. All of it. This is a great way to build a connection and relationship without having actually met them.

Reset Your Cell Phone

You know when your cell phone starts to act all sluggish, or get hot, or not keep a charge? Well, the instant reaction is to replace that sucker but resetting the one you have back to factory will make your old, slow, hot, dying phone feel like it's almost new again.

Just The Tips

Stay In Touch With Past Clients And Customers

This is so simple that it's plain stupid. If you are not in touch with your past clients, they are now someone else's prospects. Enough said.

Teach

Teach what you know to other people. Help them out. You'll get so much more back when you focus on helping people rather than making money. I have this amazing group of colleagues across the country that I participate in different events with and if they ask me to teach, I am there without hesitation. I have even hosted a mastermind event for some of them in my office and they came from coast to coast to hang out here.

Ask For A Testimonial

If you do good work, and I'm sure you all do, then ask some select customers or clients to give you a testimonial. Something in writing is great. Video is better. And there are a ton of sources where this could take place or be placed. LinkedIn, Google. Your own website, etc. This will actually help other consumers with their process, as well.

Do Video Testimonials

We already know that video is huge in letting people know who you are and what you do, en masse. So, how about letting people know about your clients' and customers' businesses? Or about businesses you frequent? How hard would it be to shoot a quick video, with your phone for example, right after walking out of dinner at your favorite restaurant? You'd get the video exposure and your client, customer and local business owner would get some exposure, as well. And you'd be doing a video which is something you need to do, anyway. Rinse and repeat, right?

Hyperlink Everything

Tag your business in social media posts. Put a Google maps link to your business location in your email signature file. Use hashtags on your posts. Whatever. Don't make it harder for people to find the people, websites, places, etc. that you want them to know about.

Keep Colleagues In Your Contact Management

I treat my respected colleagues like I would any friend, relative or client this way. And you know what? It's good for business. I have colleagues that can't always do what I do. Or they live in another part of the country and know someone who needs our services where I live. Or they are good for bouncing ideas off of or finding solutions with. Whatever the case may be, your colleagues are not competition if your mindset about them is right.

Just The Tips

Take Care Of Your Clients

I know you take care of your clients and customers. You're all great at customer service, right? But actually make this the top priority. If you take really good care of people, you'll get paid. And they will use you again. And you'll get paid. And they will refer more people to you. And you'll get paid. And then those people will use you again and refer more people to you. At it becomes a perpetual machine if you put your clients and customers first. The rest will fall into place. This is literally all you have to focus on.

Time Blocking

You have to do this. Someone once told me that happiness is a well-oiled calendar. I believe that. I have three major sections of work every day, with a thousand interruptions, of course, and some of it is time blocked in 5 minute increments. No, really. Prospecting? Time blocked. Working on client files? Time blocked. Teaching and coaching? You got it, time blocked. And I complete all three major sections, every day, before I go home at night. Depending on the interruptions, that could be at 5pm or at 8pm, but I never leave work behind.

Just The Tips

Use Your Calendar Wisely

If it's in my calendar, I will get it done. If it's on a sticky note, 50/50 odds. If I had a task list, it would never get done. I have things like take out the garbage, replace the furnace filter, and even write this book in my calendar. I also have all my prospecting in my calendar. Right down to who I am going to call and when. If you need to do something, put it in your calendar and it will get done. Stop scribbling notes or hoping you'll remember to do stuff. Hope is not a plan. Hope is what you do when a plan fails.

Check The Weather

This one is so easy and yet so many fail to do. By the time I am even considering what to put on in the morning I have gotten weather from my smart phone, my shower radio, Alexa and my bedroom television. And somehow we have droves and droves of people who had no idea that shorts and flip flops weren't going to fly when the storm moved in that afternoon.

Listen

Every good salesperson knows this. Do more listening than talking. Always. People love to talk about themselves, all of us, so let people talk. They will tell you about themselves. They will tell you the pain points you need to be solving. And now you're solving problems, not selling. You need to shut up and listen to be really good at sales.

Read

This is a great substitute for listening when you're not on the phone or in person. Read. Read people's social media posts. Read articles about your target businesses and clients. Read books written by your most trusted colleagues. Read this book. Reading is a key to growth, to learning, to selling and on and on.

Read Your Colleagues' Books

I have some amazing and revered colleagues and they have written some amazing books. Want to know what they know? Want to perform like they do? Want to be published like they are? Then get their books and get those answers.

Just The Tips

Make People Laugh

You know that old colloquialism about laughter being the best medicine? Well, it's true. People love a sense of humor. It's a major interpersonal relationship key with your significant other, your colleagues and definitely with your clients and customers.

Do Live Video

For one thing, social media loves original and organic content and there is nothing more original and organic than live video. Second, video, and especially live video, is a great way for people to really get to know you which is paramount to doing good sales work.

Just The Tips

Stalk Them A Bit

Not literally, no. It's hard to sell from jail. But just like how people love to talk about themselves, we also love to post about ourselves. Isn't that what social media as all about? So, if you're looking for an "in" then do a little research on whoever it is your trying to build a relationship with and see what they're into. Go check out a lead's Facebook page. Go see what a potential referral partner has on Instagram.

Advertising Sucks

It really does. It's expensive. It's cold. And it's ridiculous. When I see ads for my "competitors" on the TV, I laugh at how cheesy the ads are and what a waste of money it was. When I hear ads for my "competitors" on the radio, I make fun of them on social media. When I see the ad in the grocery cart, I need assistance from the grocery clerk to pick me up off the floor because I am literally ROFL. Don't advertise. Prospect instead.

Buying Leads Sucks

I cannot imagine what I have spent on "leads" over the years. Well, not in recent years but I did decades ago. This is also a cold and horrible way to generate business. You should be generating leads, not buying them. Again, do your prospecting. It's free and it's warm. Buying leads really does suck.

Just The Tips

My Wife Is Always Right

Enough said. I literally note the dates and times
when she says "You were right" since it doesn't
happen that often.

Just The Tips

Communicate With People How They Want

Some people like the phone. I know I do. Some want to text. Some like Facebook messenger. Or whatever messenger platform they like. Nonetheless, if someone wants to communicate via text, and they don't want to talk on the phone, then text them for crying out loud. Odds are, whatever you're selling, like real estate, or mortgages, or cars, provides a ton of organic and prerequisite brain damage so do what you can to minimize that for everyone. And you're more likely to have good communication with them if you're using the method they prefer.

Make Connections

One of the greatest things about being in sales is solving people's problems. That's what great sales people do. So for example, a client might call me because they need transmission repair. Now I don't know jack about transmission repair but with a database of ten thousand people, I know someone who does. So, I can make that referral, solve the transmission problem and the client and the transmission repair guy are both happy. They won't soon forget that.

Weigh Your Luggage

You have a scale at home. Use it. I weigh my luggage more than I weigh myself with it. Don't be that guy taking three sweat shirts out of his bag and putting them all on while tying a pair of shoes to his backpack so he can get in under fifty pounds, all right there at check in.

Just The Tips

Find Jobs And Employees For People

Good sales people know everyone. And they know what the people they know are doing when it comes to those looking for work, and those hiring help. So make those connections. Help people get work. Help people get quality employees. These are connections that neither party will ever forget and will make you look like a hero for a long time to come.

Drill Down Info

If you don't know what the drill down information is, find it. It's basically 50 questions about a person that if you know the answers to, they are a client for life. It's mostly social like things about the family and personal interests but there are some hard data type questions there, as well.

Just The Tips

Charge When You Can

Riding in the car? Charge your phone. Sitting next to an outlet in the restaurant? Charge your phone. Sometimes, you never know when or where that next power source is coming from, so take advantage when you can.

Get Mobile

The technology available to us enables and demands it. I carry my phone and tablet almost everywhere I go. I actually don't bother with the laptop anymore for a thousand reasons. But if I have a client or colleague that needs something quickly, like a pre-approval letter in my business, I have the ability to make that happen in a matter of minutes rather than telling someone they'll have to wait until I can get in front of a computer.

Just The Tips

Keep Track Of Who Referred Them

This is the very first thing we do. We ask who referred them either in person or on our online application. We want to know, and recognize, the people who take as good care of us as we do of them. And when I create a new file in the CRM, the very first thing I note is who referred them to us.

Just The Tips

Take And Post Pics Of Your Sales

This one probably works well for all major transactions. Cars, boats, houses, mortgages, etc. Take a picture of the happy client. Post it to social media. Your clients probably love seeing pics of their new house or car or boat. And a year from now, you'll be reminded of it giving you a trigger to reach out to your client for that "anniversary" and to see if they need another car, boat, home or mortgage or just to stay top of mind.

Just The Tips

Never Stop Working Referrals

Eventually, they all come around. Years ago, I had a client in my contact management system and after a year had no response. We took him out of that system but sometime later reached out on his birthday and BOOM, days later he called back asking to refinance his house. Never say never.

Keep In Touch, Even When They Move Away

If someone moves away, are they not going to be a client or customer anymore? Maybe. But they still know people where you are and where they just moved from. It's a small world. A mobile world. The people they still know where you are and they moved from are potential clients/customers. People they are meeting where they moved to may be moving to where you are someday, so they might be future clients/customers. Don't quit talking to people just because they moved.

Just The Tips

Make Facebook Personal And Professional

There are a number of reasons to do this. One is that nobody wants to think of you as a real estate machine. Or a car selling machine. Or a financial planning machine. They want to know that you're a human with the same experiences that they have. The other is that Facebook doesn't want you to be that machine. To them, it's personal. It's for family and friends. So, make sure you're doing both and that the majority of it is with the audience in mind, and not self-serving drivel.

Get A Data Capture App

This is a must. Capturing data, especially contact data, is crucial to building a database, which is crucial to any marketing or prospecting plans you have or will ever have. That being said, a data capture app sure beats the hell out of manual data entry into your CRM. Ever come back from an event with a stack of business cards? Wouldn't it be easier to take pictures of those instead of typing in a hundred phone numbers and email addresses yourself?

Just The Tips

Shoe Polish For Furniture

I'm not talking about getting out your shine box and buffing your ottoman but the liquid stuff that merely covers scuffs and dings works just as well on your leather furniture as it does on your leather dress shoes.

Text The Millennials

My kids don't want to talk to me. They want to text me. They want a text when it's time to go somewhere. They want a text when I am sitting out in the car ready to pick them up. They want a text when dinner is ready. So, translate that into your sales communications and use text to communicate with the people that would want to communicate via text.

Contact Information Goes Everywhere

Not just on your website. On all your web assets.
Don't make it harder for people to find the data they
need to communicate with you in whatever way they
want. Phone, email, address, Facebook page,
Instagram, whatever. Make sure that every single
method of communication with you is accessible to
them. Why would you risk losing a customer/client
because they want to email you and your email
address isn't on your website or your phone number
isn't on Facebook?

Keep Your Bio Up To Date

You bio is something you should be using on a pretty regular basis. After 15 years of being in the same role, owning the same company, I don't have a resume. What would be the point? But every time I receive an award, get something published, take on a new leadership role of some sort, etc., I update my bio and it gets used. It's on our website. It goes out with our pre-approval letters. It gets used by trade publications that run the articles I write. Just keep it up to date.

Keep Your Professional Picture Up To Date

This one cracks me up. Now, I'm not perfect about this and only do it every two or three years but I remember selling a home a decade or so ago and the listing agents stuck their sign in my yard and the photo of them had to be from 1979, I kid you not. I think the husband of this couple even had a perm in the picture. Don't be that guy. People that are going to work with you are going to see what you really look like eventually. Be on the level on every level.

Carry Business Cards

Carry them everywhere. I have a few in my wallet. I have some in my bag. I have a box in my car. I have them everywhere. This sounds Suessical, doesn't it? Seriously, don't ever deny someone your contact information. This is just like having all that data available on your web assets. Business cards are still a thing, despite what the millennial techies want.

Just The Tips

Have An Easy Website

Make sure your website is easy to use. And that it's easy to use on a mobile platform. Don't make it any more difficult than it needs to be for the average client/customer. Just because you know all the ins and outs, doesn't mean they will. Just because you like all the bells and whistles doesn't mean they will. You're not the target audience for your website so make sure you consider that audience when it comes to your website just like everything else.

Just The Tips

Have Fun Info On Your Business Cards

Business cards have been around forever. And they have been done to death. I doubt there's a single human adult on the planet that hasn't seen a business card. And most of them are god awful boring. Obviously, the information that's required for people to contact you is a must but do something interesting with it. We do all our social media avenues on ours, for example. I'm just as happy to let someone find me on Facebook or LinkedIn as having them call or email me.

Just The Tips

Headsets

The good news is that these have become more and more affordable over time. The bad news is that I still buy a ton of them. I have wireless, binaural Bluetooth ones, and monaural Bluetooth ones (in my bag and my car, for sure) and a wireless one attached to my desk phone, and an array of corded ones, and on and on. But the ability to be hands free in the car, on the computer, basically everywhere, is priceless to me. I never could stand the phone wedged between my head and shoulder.

Fax To Email

If you're actually still using a fax, let me know and I will send you the 20 year old rolls of thermal paper gathering dust in our supply room. Now, I know people still fax, and we still receive them, but our "fax number" actually just ports over to a system that automatically converts the faxes to PDF and emails them to the entire team. As far as sending a fax goes, well…we would have no idea how to do that so it's a good thing we don't have to.

Voicemail To Email

I'm not much for using my cell phone unless I am out of the office, and since I am in the office most waking and all business hours, I really don't use it much. Nobody calls me on it. But if I am out of the office and someone leaves a message there, I get the message immediately because we have it set up to email voice messages as they come in. And it's a media file, not just a notification, so I can play it on my phone like any other MP3, and not have to call and check my messages. What a PITA that used to be, huh?

Just The Tips

Put The Cap Back On The Pen

Best case, you end up with a small mark on your hand. Worst case, you ruin an article of clothing. Either way, the two seconds it takes to click or put the cap back on a pen is well worth it.

Just The Tips

Apply For Industry Awards

We see this all the time in the mortgage and real estate industries but many publications across all of them will actually solicit for nominees for their different awards. Some of them I see and have a colleague or team member nominate me. Some I never see and someone has already nominated me. Some I wouldn't have even known about if not for some amazing colleague watching my back. But when you see them, apply for them. You never know, you might be picked and it adds real value to your credibility.

Just The Tips

Personal Success

Someone once asked me how I define if I am
financially successful and I have three rules. One,
if I want three dozen rolls of toilet paper stacked up
on the shelf above my toilet, I can do that. Two, I
never think twice about the additional cost of the
guacamole, even when the Chipotle employee
asks. And three, I refuse to drive around and
around looking for the cheaper parking spot and will
always take the more convenient one.

Just The Tips

Connect Your Social Media Accounts

I know this seems like common sense but it's not that easy if you're not tech savvy. It is possible to link Facebook to Instagram. And LinkedIn to Twitter. And Facebook to Twitter. And Twitter to Tumblr. And Instagram to Tumblr. And on and on. It will save you time when posting across multiple platforms and it will help with your branding as all the pictures, logos, copy, etc. will be synonymous.

Just The Tips

Watch Glen Gary Glenn Ross and Boiler Room

There are a ton, well, not a ton, but a dozen or so great sales movies. These two are the bomb. Watch them if you haven't already. If you have, watch them again. And there are a ton of others like Jerry Maguire and The Wolf of Wall Street, and even Wall Street. Google a list, figure out what genre captures you, what era interests you and watch some of these great sales movies.

Reach Out At Tax Time

Taxes. One of life's certainties, right? Well put this inevitability to good use for yourself and do your clients/customers a solid. Every major purchase and financial event they had last year probably had some tax implications. So reach out to them and see if there is anything they need or any documents you can supply to them, or even directly to their tax preparer, to help with that process. You'll have an excuse to reach out and stay top of mind. You'll be helping them out with a horrible task. You might add a new tax preparer to your contact database. The benefits are huge for everyone. Do this.

Just The Tips

Be Consistent In Your Lead Generation

Whatever you're doing in your prospecting, marketing, lead generation, etc., make sure you are doing it constantly and consistently. That's the only way it's going to work. You can't part time it. You can't half ass it. You have to do whatever it is you're doing every day for a long time in order to get any results.

Be Consistent In Your Processes

Make sure your internal processes are consistent. That every client and customer gets the same process every time. That everyone on your team has the same process on every deal. That your follow up is the same with every contact. Again, consistency is a big tool in building a repeat and referral business.

Just The Tips

Be Consistent In Everything

Be consistent in your work. Be consistent in your relationships. Be consistent in your sleep and exercise routines. Be consistent with your diet. Be consistent in your every aspect of your life and your success will be consistent, too.

Wrong Numbers Equal New Contacts

You want to see someone with MAD phone skills? I know people who know how to convert wrong numbers. That's the pinnacle of phone sales, I s#&t you not. Now, I've always been good at turning the tables on telemarketers trying to sell me something but to do it with a total stranger that hadn't even considered whatever it is you're selling...that's impressive. At a minimum, have a nice chat and maybe add a new contact to your database.

Three Songs

Pick out three songs to listen to every day. One that reminds you of how loved and appreciated you are. I use my wedding song. One that really makes you feel like you're in your "zone". I always had a few of these to listen to before I got in the race car. And one that makes you feel powerful and unstoppable. I'm not giving you my three because I don't want to taint your three.

Just The Tips

Save Everything.

I'm not talking about pack ratting or hoarding. I'm talking about it from a technological standpoint. I am a digital pack rat. Save every email. Save every document. Save every picture. Every video. The storage capability of computers today is virtually limitless, especially if you actually do it virtually, so take advantage. You'll never have to worry about missing a document, needing to call up an email, or wanting to watch a video again. Just save it all and you'll never have to worry about it again.

Just The Tips

Make Good Use Of Your ADD

It's no secret that most people in sales have some form or degree of ADD. So, take advantage of it. If you get bored or lose focus with one particular task, put it down, and work on another one. When you get back on track, go back and pick it up again. The neat thing about most sales gigs is that it's multi-faceted. There are a number of different things you need to do each day, so you can rotate them around.

Extra Batteries And Battery Packs

We've all been there. The battery on your phone says 8% and you're about to board a plane or you're going to be somewhere with no outlet in sight. Some cell phones still have the ability to replace the battery, so keep an extra one charged. If you can't do that, a backup battery is just as good. Keep them charged and keep them handy.

Just The Tips

Contacts - Relationships - Friends - Clients

This is the path to successful sales. You have to meet people and make contacts. Then you have to take those contacts and build relationships. The better relationships will develop into friendships. And finally, friends become clients.

Just The Tips

Get A Good Cell Phone Mount

I don't care what you're using your phone for in the car but whether it's talking on the phone, using Waze or Google Maps or anything else, having a good mount that keeps it in place, and helps you keep your eyes on the road, is priceless. Do what you can to make that time in the car safer and more productive.

You Need And Can Afford An Assistant

You really do. Even if it's part time at 20 hours a week. Even if it's only $15 an hour. If you took all the menial crap off your plate to the tune of 80 hours and $1200 a month, could you use that 80 hours more productively to where you could earn another $1200 in that time? So, figure out the stuff that you either hate doing or doesn't make you any money and pay someone else to do it. You'll even be giving someone else a job so it's a win-win.

There's Plenty To Go Around

Seriously. If you're of the scarcity mindset in your sales gig that you cannot be forthcoming and helpful with other salespeople in your arena, you're in the wrong gig. If you're good at what you do, there is plenty of business to be had. And being open and helpful with other people to make them more successful will actually help you, not hurt you. I cannot imagine how many other mortgage people I have taught to, coached and pulled back my proverbial curtain for in an effort to raise the bar in my industry without merely focusing on me and my wallet.

Put Personal Stuff On Social Media

Social media is just that, it's social. Nobody wants to see only posts about the houses or cars you're selling. Selling requires making sure people know who you are and what you do. The what you do is easy and boring. Use social media to share who you are. Be personal. Be human. Be relatable. People want to learn about who you are, not just what you do. That stuff is important but remember the old know, like and trust adage? You can't get that without really letting people see who you are on a personal level.

Just The Tips

Exercise

Yes, I admittedly suck at this one most of the time but you have got to exercise for a thousand reasons. You'll live longer. You'll feel better. You'll sleep better. You'll blow off steam. You'll be more productive in your work. And it will be something that can help you have a more balanced schedule, too.

Put Triggers In Place

You all know the simplicity of "If A, then B". Well, implement this into your business. A good sales example would be something like; "If the sale is made, then add the buyer to our customer email drip campaign." We use a ton of these in our business, so that we don't have to remember certain, individual steps every time something occurs in the sales cycle.

Just The Tips

Take Good Care Of Your Cords And Chargers

It drives me crazy when I see someone pull a rat's nest of abused and tangled headphones out of their pocket. Wrap that stuff up nicely when you're done with it and not only will you save the time and headache of having to detangle that mess, but the headphones, or charger cable, or whatever, will last longer, too.

Donate In Clients' Names

You're going to do some charitable giving, so why not make it mean even more than it already does? Every year, we ask our past clients to nominate their favorite charity, and we donate to that charity, in their name, for every single person that asks us to make a donation.

Just The Tips

Tip Everyone

Throw the porter a few bucks at curbside and they'll likely put a priority tag on your bag so it's the first one off the plane and waiting for you at baggage claim when you get there. Slip the maître d' a fin and you'll likely get a better table faster. Take care of the flight attendant that has the worst "server" job on the globe. Let people know you acknowledge them and appreciate their work. You want people to do that for you, right?

Just The Tips

Like Everything

Want to build a relationship from scratch? Start by liking that person's social media stuff. In fact, like everyone's stuff. Then maybe make some comments. Perhaps send a direct message. Find things you have in common. This is basic, cornerstone, getting to know you activity with a twist for the current way we all communicate with each other.

Just The Tips

Multiple Port USB Chargers

Not only will you have the added benefit of being able to charge all your stuff at the same time but this will make you an airport hero. I carry a very small one that has 4 USB ports for one plug and if I whip that out at the airport when outlets are limited, and offer it up to the next three people struggling to find an outlet when their cell phone is on the brink of dying, I am their hero.

Just The Tips

Make Sure Your Bio Is Personal and Professional

Make sure your bio has personal stuff in it. I kid you not I had a client, who is now a good friend, decide to reach out to me and work with me because he knew I was a hockey fan. He saw my volunteer work with the Colorado Avalanche on my LinkedIn profile and that was enough for him. We've been friends ever since and still go to hockey games together every season.

Sly Broadcast

I'm sure I already mentioned Sly Dial and how useful it can be in your sales business but if you think that idea is cool, check out Sly Broadcast. You can drop the same message into unlimited voice mail boxes at one time, instead of just one at a time. We use this one for all kinds of things from clients, to leads, to referral partners.

Just The Tips

Video Is A Great Way To Communicate

How many people do you see using Facetime? Or maybe you use it. Or maybe you like the Facebook video messenger service. Or perhaps text messages with embedded videos. I could go on, obviously. The point is, video rocks. Did you know there's more video being uploaded to the internet every 30 days than network television produced the last 30 years? I'm sure I talk about video a dozen times in these tips so am I getting through yet?

Just Remember "CLA"

CLA is clients, leads and advocates. Someone who has done business with you. Someone who is going to do business with you. And someone who is going to refer business to you. These are the top "categories" of people you should be contacting, prospecting to, marketing to or whatever you want to call it.

Get A Caller ID App

Yes, I know your phone has caller ID. That's not what I'm talking about. I am talking about a 3rd party app that lets every other user on the globe help you with identifying callers. I like True Caller, myself. So, when a robocall or those awesome IRS, "we're coming to arrest you right now" calls go to anyone using the app, they can identify it as a scam, or anything else, and then every other user gets that information when their phone rings. But remember, telemarketers need what you're selling, too.

Just The Tips

Have Systems And Use Them

For the most part, every good business has good business practices. When I say that, I mean the ability to take on projects or programs, massage and manipulate those tactics to suit their business, implement and automate them as much as possible, and do it the same way, every time. Having good systems in place is paramount to sales success. If you're winging it, you're suffering, I promise. If you have good systems in place, you will get busier. The better your systems are, the easier that business will be to handle.

Just The Tips

Wear Your Seatbelt On The Airplane

I know this seems like common sense to most of us but I travel a lot so I see a lot of stupid travelers. Ever been on an airplane that has a very brief, but very sudden, change in altitude? The kind of change that makes your stomach flip like a roller coaster? Ever see the unbuckled passenger get bumped into the bottom of the overhead compartment when it happens? Ouch. You don't want to be that guy.

Promote Your Colleagues And Competitors

I've already mentioned how important collaboration with your colleagues and competitors is but so is promoting them. If someone tells me they are using another lender that I know and like, I will tell them I know and like them and that they are in good hands. The same with your employees/team. I constantly boast to everyone, even in my voice mail greeting and email auto replies about how amazing they are and that they are smarter than I am and know more than I do.

"Adam" Asked Me To..."

This one is HUGE. Every phone call. Every email. Every bit of communication originating from my office or from my team starts with "Adam asked me to". I asked them to call. I asked them to email. I asked them to write. Whatever. I don't have time to handle every call and email personally but I want my clients, colleagues and referral partners to know that I am thinking about them and their deals all the time.

Sleep

Sleep is critical. Good sleep leads to good everything else. It makes you mentally sharp. It enables better sales skills. It makes you feel better physically. On and on. Trust me on this. I know. I'm a Viking when it comes to sleeping. And eating. But that's another story.

Just The Tips

Only Do Things You Like To Do

This one is simple. Identify all the things you do and if you don't like doing them, pay someone else to do them.

Just The Tips

Only Do Things You're Good At

Here's another one. Once you've identified all the things you do, if you suck at something that has to get done, pay someone else who's better than you to do it.

Just The Tips

Only Do Things That Make You Money

This another place you need some help. Of all the
things you do, if it's not $100 an hour work or $200 an
hour work, then pay someone else to do it. Only do
things during the day that you like, you're good at, or
make you money and pay someone to do the rest.

Just The Tips

Marker Boards

I know this sounds antiquated but only because it is. I mean, how long have these things existed? Didn't Alec Baldwin use one in Glengarry Glen Ross? Anyway, what's old is new again and these are still great tools. I think we have one in every office and conference room for all kinds of different reasons. Pipelines, notes, shopping lists, task lists, whatever. Have and use them wisely, and you'll get great mileage out of them, too.

Find Reasons To Reach Out

There are always reasons to reach out to people to stay top of mind. A good example for us was the Equifax data breach in recent years. What a great reason for a mortgage lender or real estate agent or car dealer to contact all his clients to discuss what happened, what their options going forward were, and to make sure they knew that you want to play an active role in protecting their borrowing power.

Just The Tips

LogMeIn And Splashtop

These are only two of what may be a bunch of apps in this arena but having the ability to remote in to different computers from anywhere and everywhere on the globe is awesome. I don't even carry a computer anymore. Just my tablet. If I am at home, I use the computer and LogMeIn to remote into my office computer. And if I am on the road, I use Splashtop on my tablet to do the same.

Just The Tips

Call Everyone. Even When It's Not For Business

The bottom line is that whatever you're selling, odds are everyone needs it, or knows someone who does. I have people in my call list that will never use me for a mortgage but know dozens, if not hundreds, of people that would, and do.

Just The Tips

Know What The DISC Is

DISC is a personality profile system. There are several similar models but know what it means. Knowing about people's personalities will help you with clients, colleagues, employees and even your significant other. If you can recognize some the traits of each type, you will see those traits in people and it will help you communicate with them in a way they will be more receptive to.

Just The Tips

If You Don't Know, Say So

Under no circumstance do you make things up. If someone asks you a question that you do not know the answer to, tell them you will find out or that you will ask and get back to them. Do not tell them something that may or may not be true. You're always better off going and getting the knowledge and reporting back than you are making things up and looking like an as$#@le.

Just The Tips

Kids' Birthdays And Wedding Anniversaries

Pay extra attention to these. I know I am going to have thousands of people reach out to me in some manner or another on my own birthday but when someone knows my kids' birthdays, or my wedding anniversary, and acknowledges that, it goes a long way. Put those dates in your calendar when you come across them.

Just The Tips

A Clear Cell Phone Case

This is a great trick for temporarily storing things that you need intact. I learned this one at Disneyland, actually. I don't know if you've been recently, but they use a small paper ticket that is bar coded with all kinds of information, including a picture of you. If it's a multiple day pass, the need to keep it in good condition is even more important. So, I stick it in my clear cell phone case. Their scanners can still read it through the clear plastic and it doesn't get damaged. This works great for sporting event tickets and concert tickets, too.

Just The Tips

Your Assistants Should Do Personal Stuff

This one still bothers me some, and I try not to do it very often but it is a good tip. The time you spend running to the bank or car wash is probably a lot more valuable than the money you're paying an assistant. Even a step beyond that, having someone to clean your house, cut your grass or do your grocery shopping can fit in the same formula and even free up more valuable personal and family time.

You Are A Salesperson

I know most of you reading this freely admit that but I have news for all you mortgage originators, real estate agents, financial planners, insurance agents and so on; you are salespeople. Being an expert about your business is only half your gig. You also need to be generating business and that is a sales gig. You can know everything there is to know about premiums and deductibles but if you're not bringing in business, it doesn't matter. You may as well go and learn everything about special sauce and sesame seed buns at that point.

Just The Tips

Keep Learning Your Profession

Continuing education, your education, is huge. And learning is a lifelong task. Granted, most of us have required continuing education but that's not what I mean. I do my federal and state required continuing education every year but it isn't helping me generate more business. Find great classes. Go to cool conferences. Get great books by other sales people. Never stop learning this stuff. If will make you better at sales and it will provide more value to your clients and customers.

Back Up Your Contact Database

Like my mortgage company, most salespeople's greatest asset is their contact database. It's important for a hundred reasons like marketing and prospecting so treat it as such. My database is on my computer, my phone, my tablet, and is backed up both locally and remotely. I'm not taking any chances with my greatest asset.

Just The Tips

Make Another Backup Of Your Database

See my previous tip. Once you have your contact database, likely your greatest asset, backed up, make another back up. Trust me on this one.

Just The Tips

Support Your Clients' And Colleagues' Kids

One of the greatest examples of this I can think of was a referral partner sending me a picture of our "ad" in the program for his kid's school ballet program while he was at the ballet recital, thanking me for being supportive of his child. I think it cost us twenty bucks and the results were priceless.

Just The Tips

Learn How To Depressurize Your Ears

Scuba divers know this one but I live in a pretty landlocked place so there aren't a lot of those. But we do have a lot of air travelers and the same principle applies. Major changes in depth, or altitude, can wreak havoc on the pressure in your head. Learn how to depressurize your ears and you'll be able to give yourself instant relief when the pressure builds up.

Just The Tips

Your Best Competitors Are That For A Reason

You know that guy in your business that is just crushing it? There's a reason he's crushing it. Look and see what he's doing. Follow him on social media. See what reviews he's getting from his clients and customers. Buy his book. Read the articles he's published. Not only will it help you crush it but let's remember what they say about imitation.

The Biggest Transactions Of People's Lives

Nine times out of ten, those of you reading this book, are dealing with the largest transactions of people's lives. Real estate agents, absolutely. Mortgage lenders, you bet. Car salespeople, highly likely. Financial planners, a good chance. Take good care of your clients. Put them first. Focus on solving their problems and accomplishing their goals and the rest will fall into place. But make no mistake, you are being trusted with the largest transactions of people's lives. Treat it as such.

Just The Tips

Double Up On Hotel Keys

Hotel keys are an even bigger pain in the ass than my usual keys. They don't always work, they're easy to lose and other than a potential card key for work for some of you, who else uses this medium? So, I always get two hotel keys, knowing one will potentially fail and stick one in my wallet or bag just in case I lose the first one, assuming they both work, anyway.

Just The Tips

Help The People That Didn't Work With You

I assure you people always regret not working with us when they go somewhere else. A lot of them we hear back from, and we even get some apologies, and we know there are a ton that are too embarrassed to discuss it, as well. And that's fine, too. But those people still need your help because the other guy sucked at doing his job. And those people are going to buy another car. They are going to buy another home someday. They will refinance their mortgage. And they know a bunch of people that will do all of the above. So, don't lose sight of the job of taking care of people. It's not about a paycheck. It's about a long, rewarding, fulfilling career. You all know you always get more than you give.

Just The Tips

There Are No Such Things As Sales Emergencies

Nobody is going to die today because of an issue with their mortgage, or their home sale, or their life insurance physical (well, actually that might do it). The point is that setting boundaries is an important part of your process. If clients are calling or pinging you at all hours of the night, and you're answering or responding, you're enabling that behavior. You're a human being with a life, a family, personal stuff going on, etc. so don't be dragged into that.

Just The Tips

Send Yourself Emails

This is one of my single greatest reminder tricks I use. I email myself little notes all the time. I come up with an idea for my blog or a video, I email myself. I come up with a tip for this book, I email myself. I need a reminder of something to do when I get to the office, I email myself. I get a message from someone via text or Facebook, etc., I screenshot it and email it to myself. I'll bet I do this at least once a day.

Go To Open Houses

Here is an opportunity to meet or spend some time with a colleague, a potential referral partner, another great salesperson or maybe a new friend. And you'll be saving them from the doldrums that open houses can be. I've done some for my referral partners over the years and they can be BORING AF. And get creative with your visit. I like shooting live video with them talking about the house and themselves. Or maybe bring them one of those swag backup cell phone batteries in case they forgot. Nothing wrong with a simple cup of coffee, either.

Spend Time With Successful People

People are the direct result of the five people they spend the most time with, right? So, who do you want to be? Someone successful. Then spend time with the people you want to be like and learn how they have the successes and accomplishments that you want. That goes for family, significant others, colleagues, teams, etc. Remember, success isn't just a monetary measurement.

CRMs

You know what the best CRM is? The one you will use. I cannot believe how many people I see that have no semblance to their database. Some of it is in their phone. Some of it is on the computer. Some of it is in Google. Some of it is on a spreadsheet. A spreadsheet? Come on, people. Get a CRM and use it. Keep your contact database, likely your greatest asset, in check and be smart about it.

Just The Tips

Hire People Smarter Than You

This is something I do well and take great pride in. My entire team is smarter than I am. And they know more than I do. And each of them has a very specific job and knowledge base so they are very, very skilled and knowledgeable at that particular job. I think Steve Jobs said something like; "we don't hire smart people and tell them what to do. We hire smart people and have them tell us what to do."

Just The Tips

Doctors And Lawyers Versus Breakfast

Doctors and lawyers aren't really "shopped". Well, I'm not talking about the bus bench PI lawyers but their method of client attraction and advertising leads to that possibility. I'm talking about the trusted authorities, not the people who provide a service or product that is the same at Denny's or Village Inn. Be like the lawyer or doctor and having a strict repeat and referral business will enable that.

The Hamburger Versus The Expert

How many times have you lost a sale because someone else was doing it cheaper? Exactly. That makes you a commodity in that way. Not a lot of difference between a 99 cent McDonald's hamburger and an 89 cent Burger King hamburger except for the dime. People will go for saving the dime every time if the product is bottom of the barrel and a dime makes a difference. Have a better product, better service and be a better expert and they'll never choose the dime.

Write Reviews For Your Colleagues

A portion of the reviews we get, and the ones we give, come from or are for colleagues and competitors. I will always write something nice about an agent, or title company, or wholesaler when they deserve it and I will even write ones about the worthy competitors, too. And they reciprocate, of course. We already know writing reviews is a great way to get reviews and this group should be included in that process. And even if they don't write one for you, you're still the bigger person.

Lock Boxes For Ditching Keys

I am not a big fan of carrying keys but I cannot seem to get away from it. Between the cars, the office, the house and on and on, I feel like a custodian some days from all the keys I carry around. But old school real estate lockboxes are a great way to ditch some of that. I keep one mounted at home, another at the office, one on the bumper of my RV, and by doing so I get to lighten my key load.

Find The Rentals Near You

This one is really great for the mortgage and real estate people, especially. The house next door to me has been a rental the entire 16 years I've lived there and I have probably turned a dozen transactions off the tenants becoming homeowners, refinancing their homes, and even selling and buying new ones. Once I figured that out, I found two other rentals on my block and always make friends with those tenants, too.

Find Neighborhood Groups

Your neighbors are a great source of business if you're involved with them. Neighborhood groups, both live and digital, block parties, HOA meetings and gathering places like the pool or recreation centers are all good places to be social with your neighbors. I even volunteer as a neighborhood watch captain and host an annual block party that my company sponsors. This is a great way to build your audience and even become a hyperlocal expert.

Replicate Yourself

This is an ideal and necessary mentality in scaling your business. Figure out what you do, and do well, and find other people that can do it and do it well. If you can clone you that way, your growth and success will be exponential to the same degree.

Replicate Your Business

Having systems in place that make the process for your clients and customers, as well as the other professionals involved in a transaction, the same every time will not only make their perception better but it will make your life easier. If you do things the same way every time and if your team does the same tasks every time, the results will be the same every time.

Have Some Canned Responses

I hate the "elevator speech" but it does have some value. Remember, we're all conditioned to ask stupid questions like "what do you do?" and "how's work" so have some canned responses for that questions that will help you generate leads with your answers.

Share Your Knowledge

If you're in sales you've had a ton of training and education, even if you're brand new to whatever you're selling. Don't deny people that knowledge especially when you don't think you have anything to offer in that arena because you're a newbie. I often have to tell new real estate agents that don't want to sound "salesy" to their friends that they need to change their mindset about it and shame on them for holding back that wealth of knowledge they just gained in real estate school. Your clients, customers, friends and family are relying on you to keep them informed and educated about your industry/

Screenshots

This may be one of the greatest things your cell phone can do. A colleague messages you a lead on Facebook, screenshot. A client texts you an image of something you need from them, screenshot. You need a reminder of something you saw an image of, screenshot. And just like my email tip for reminders, I will send myself the screenshots and there they are waiting in my inbox for me to address the next time I am at the computer.

Name Badges

We don't need no stinkin' badges. Yeah, you do. If you're in real estate, or mortgages, or anything where there is BTB networking, get one. And wear it. You, and everyone else, meet a ton of people all the time. At least you should be. And I am sure you can't remember the names of everyone you meet. Well, neither do they. So, make it easier on them to remember who you are with a name badge.

Just The Tips

Networking Events For Others' Businesses

I once heard this coined as "netweaving" but the general practice is to do networking events to help someone else's business. When you get to a networking event, find someone and learn about their business. Then, spend the rest of the event trying to find ways to network with everyone else that will help that first person's business. I promise you that they will never forget it and we all know we get more than we give, when we give. This is a good way to give.

Just The Tips

If You Dream About Peeing

Odds are good that you really have to go.
Hopefully you can wake yourself up and go so you
can save some money on rubber sheets

All Contacts Matter

It's pretty likely that you sell something that everyone is going to need or want, eventually. Now, that doesn't mean that they can all afford it or will buy it, but they might want it. And they might know people who can afford it and will buy it. Don't discount the contact that might have the potential to refer you customer or clients even if they are never going to be one.

Just The Tips

If You Don't Ask

It's an automatic "no". No matter what the question is,
if you don't ask it, the answer is "no". Ask for the sale.
Ask for the raise. Ask your significant other to do that
thing you like in bed. If you don't ask, it's an
automatic "no".

Meet NEW People At Networking Events

Yes, I am guilty of this, too. I can't believe how many times I've done this and how often I see other people do this but you show up for a networking event, see some people you know, and you go hang out with them the whole time. Don't do that. The whole idea is to meet new people and build your network, your contacts, your relationships, and your audience. Go meet some new people for crying out loud.

Identify The Best Types Of Referral Partners

Spend some time figuring out where your best referral business comes from. For me, it's past clients. I have a few certain circles and if someone calls me and says they were referred from with that group of friends, family, coworkers, etc. then I know they are also going to be great to work with. Once you've identified where your best referrals come from, you can sharpen your prospecting and marketing to help make sure you're getting the referrals you want.

Just The Tips

A Napkin Can Save Your Pants

It's no secret that I make messes like a toddler. I have discovered that if I am diligent about putting a napkin my lap, I greatly lower my risk of walking around all afternoon with the residue from whatever I had at lunch.

Keep Stamped Thank You Notes

Just keep a few around. Maybe even in your car. And then when the moment strikes that you want to thank someone, you won't have to remember to do it later. You can scratch out a quick thank you note and drop it in the next mailbox you see.

Just The Tips

Use The Same Images Across Social Media

Your logo. Your profile picture. Whatever. Make sure those images are the same across all your web assets. It will help people recognize you and your branding. That kind of synonymity will pay dividends by getting ingrained in peoples' minds.

Post Your Community Service Stuff

Let people know you're all about your community. LinkedIn even has a section for volunteer and philanthropic work. This is along the lines of letting people know who you are and what you're about. You never know, someone interested in the same volunteerism that you are might become a good friend and client/customer someday.

Post For The Greater Good

Do not post material on social media about how great you are. Or about how wonderful your company is. People see right through that garbage. Make sure what you're posting is for the greater good, is solid content and is NOT self-serving.

Just The Tips

Put The Phone Away At Night

Remember as kids the old adage about how we shouldn't be doing our homework where we sleep? That there's some supposed psychological toll to that? Well, the same goes as adults. Don't put the phone, one of your major work tools, under your pillow at night. Or even on the nightstand. When it's time to shut down, shut it down. There is no emergency in your sales job where somebody is going to die at 2:00 am if you don't respond to a text or email before morning.

Just The Tips

Be Like The Dentist

I'm not talking about inflicting great pain here. What I mean is think about their office…everyone has a different job, a set task, does it well, and nobody overlaps. Reception does the receiving. Hygienists do the cleaning. Billing does well, the billing. And you see the dentist for 5 minutes in the whole process. Use that as a model for your business.

Be A Calming Force

Whatever it is your client or customer is buying, it's likely something that can add some stress. A house, a mortgage, a car, insurance, whatever. It definitely angries up the blood a tad. So, be a calming force. A voice of reason. A rock. Don't add to that stress but rather smooth the waves and help everyone keep a level head.

Firing Clients

I know firing a client is tough, especially when you're new to whatever it is you're selling. But this is an occasional necessity. After 20 years in mortgages, I have some freedoms that some of you do not yet but if a client is being rude or abusive, or isn't performing in a manner necessary to get their loan done, we probably have to fire them. But the time you just saved by doing it will free up time to go find more clients.

Just The Tips

Ask For The Business

This one is simple. You can't just show up. You can't just say you're in sales. You can't just go to networking events. You can't just give great pitches. You can't just have a kick ass product. You can't just make killer presentations. You have to ask for the business. So, ask for the business.

Just The Tips

Take Time To Meet The People On Airplanes

You're already stuck with that person or people for a few hours anyway, right? They might be a potential customer or client. They might be a highly knowledgeable colleague. I sat next to a guy from a nearby city en route to a conference we were both attending and had two of the most productive hours of my life talking about prospecting ideas and I've even implemented a few of his ideas. It was so amazing that a total stranger sitting behind us complimented us after landing on how impressed he was that we could have that conversation.

Just The Tips

Don't Take Business Away From Someone Else

In essence, sales people are all self-employed small business people and wake up every day unemployed. Making sales is how we feed our families and how we pay our teams so they can feed their families. Now, if you're looking to win a piece of business because you have a better price, or service, or whatever, then I get that. But to steal business from a competitor for that reason alone. Uh uh. Would you want someone to do that to you? It'll come back to you, I promise.

Don't Underestimate The Power Of Music

Denver has really only had one, great, local, historic concert promoter and I grew up with his kids. I got to spend a little time with him when playing at his house, etc. and while I didn't understand it then, I do now. He said something like; everything you do, do it with music. And he was right. Music makes everything better.

Just The Tips

Delete Old Contacts From Your Cycle

Have old contacts in your CRM that either don't use you or refer people to you? Well, stop that. Do some maintenance on your database and stop "campaigning" to the people that aren't going to vote for you, anyway.

Just The Tips

Use Facebook For Picture And Video Storage

I don't have unlimited storage on my phone or computer but in essence, Mark Zuckerberg does. Thanks Mark for letting me use your servers to save all my pictures and videos at no cost. I appreciate it.

Educate your clients and customers

Sales isn't about closing deals. Sales is about educating people. Make sure they understand the pitfalls of buying a home. Make sure they know which side the fuel port is on that new car. Make sure they grasp how long they're going to have that mortgage insurance. Educating people is so valuable in showing you care about the customer and about your profession.

Just The Tips

Carry On, Check Back

Ah, the great debate about whether to check or carry on your luggage. Well, if I am traveling somewhere, I am taking a limited amount of my belongings and am really going to need them when I get there. I kind of want to make sure the bag gets there when I get there. For the return trip, the majority of my belongings are already at home so not having my luggage for a few days isn't going to be a big deal.

Be Persistent

Not taking no for an answer might be a little excessive but I have had plenty of clients over the years tell me no, even go work with someone else, and eventually come back. If you're consistent and persistent in everything you do, your business will be, too. Keep reaching out to past leads. Keep following up with the referral partners you want to work with. Keep on keeping on and you'll get the results you want.

Just The Tips

Keep Toilet Paper In Your Car

Just trust me on this one. Better to have it and not need it than need it and not have it.

Just The Tips

Find Some Great Authors

You'd be amazed at who has written a book. Or trade related magazine articles. We don't really publicize nonfiction these days because of it, so there is a wealth of knowledge out there that you don't even know about. Google some of the people in your industry that you aspire to be like and I'll bet a lot of them are authors. And I'd bet their writings would help you in your business, too.

Just The Tips

Do Video Because People On Screen Are Important

Isn't that true? Aren't the people on TV important for some reason? The people in movies? Admit it, you even think the people you see on YouTube are important. Aren't you important? Well, you might be seen as such if you're doing video as that seems to be human nature for us to regard people on screen that way.

Just The Tips

Do Videos

I've probably already covered this in this book but it's too important not to drill into your head a million times. Do videos. Do Facebook live videos. Do recorded videos. Do Instagram TV. Do Snapchat videos. I do not care. Just do them. This is a cheap and easy way to make sure people really know who you are and what you do.

Just The Tips

Do More Videos

The key to doing videos, like anything, is to keep doing it. Wash, rinse, repeat. Don't do a couple of videos and expect to be an overnight YouTube star and see success. Keep doing them.

Just The Tips

Restaurants Have Really Hot Water

They have to. They have to basically scald their dishes clean to be sanitary so they typically have hotter water than anything we're used to at home, office, hotel, etc. So, be careful when washing your hands in a restaurant because it's supposed be ridiculously hot water.

Be Flexible With Clients And Customers

Accommodate your clients and customers as best you can. Someone wants to talk in the evening. Do that. Someone prefers communication via text. Do that. Someone needs to meet with you on Saturday. Do that, too. Most likely whatever it is your selling creates some amount of brain damage to buy. Try to minimize that for them and accommodate the little things.

Nobody Is Going To Die

No matter what you're selling, unless it's defibrillators, there are likely no life or death emergencies in your business. It may seem like it, especially to your clients and customers, but it's not. Nobody is going to die. Don't contribute to the chaos and panic a lot of large transactions cause for buyers and sellers. Be a calming force. Remember, nobody is going to die.

Call Your Mother

Put it in your calendar if you have to, but call her. She wiped your ass, for crying out loud. And she isn't going to be around forever. In fact, it wouldn't kill you to do this from time to time with all your relatives.

Advertising And Marketing Versus Prospecting

It's no secret that I am a huge proponent of zero cost marketing. There are so many tools available to sales people that paying for advertising or marketing isn't necessary any longer. Good prospecting, good social media work, good phone skills, good relationships and a thousand other things that don't cost a dime trump the things that do. Don't advertise. Prospect.

Just The Tips

Think Before You Advertise

If you're going to advertise your business, you really need to do your homework. There are so many ways to advertise and so many companies willing to take your money, that the possibilities are virtually limitless. Really analyze your ROI before spending money you may be wasting. Find out what other people advertising in those mediums are getting out of it. See if they're satisfied. Figure out if it's unique or is the same old boring bus bench and grocery cart advertising.

Closed Captioning

I love closed captioning. I love it because my kids get to read what they're hearing on the television and gain some context, see word spellings, proper grammar (well, not all television has that) and sentence structure. And I don't miss any lines, especially when it's foreign, but still in English like movies done with British, Scottish, Irish, Australian actors, etc.

Have A Call To Action

Make your marketing and prospecting interactive. People want to be involved. People want to give opinions. People want to take polls (easy ones, anyway). People want to participate, so let them. Get them to take action so that you can respond and interact. Don't market like a dead or dying fish and just flop around on the ground until you've completely wasted those marketing dollars and efforts.

Internships

Interns are amazing. And they are a great resource for when you need some help. Young adults these days are eager, hard-working, well educated, and they are struggling with the job market. This is a symbiotic win-win relationship. If you need help, get an intern. If you're a college student looking for work in a potential, lucrative, long-term career, find a role with a real estate agent, or a mortgage lender, or an insurance office or a financial planner and so on.

Just The Tips

Learn How To Get Through Airport Security

This one drives me nuts and if you travel a lot it probably drives you nuts, too. Recently for an outbound flight, the three people in line in front of me for TSA pre-check were not TSA approved. The three people in front of them stalled taking off their shoes and belts because they don't know what pre-check means and the guy behind me got his bag flagged in the x-ray machine meaning mine hadn't come off the belt yet so I had to wait on him. Please don't be these people.

Just The Tips

Everything Is A Contact Database

Facebook is a contact database. Instagram is a contact database. Your contact database is a contact database. You've got have a contact database, or lots of them, for any marketing and prospecting so consider what your social media contact databases look like and how those audiences can benefit you.

Pets Are A Great Way To Connect

People who love pets love other people who love pets. Even more specifically, people who love dogs love other people who love dogs. And people who love cats love other people who love cats. I have both and I can safely say that I have likely made hundreds of connections, contacts, etc. just from the dog park and obedience school. My dogs, past and present, are definitely responsible for some of my sales.

Just The Tips

Find Your Tribes

Are you a vegan? Are you into CrossFit? Are you a video gamer? Whatever it is you're into, make sure you're putting that out there and connecting with people that are into whatever it is you're into. This is a great way to make like-minded connections, build relationships and eventually make clients.

Just The Tips

Remote Starters

In case I hadn't mentioned it, I live in Colorado. And it gets hot here. And it gets cold here. And my cars have remote starters. AC is the summer, heat in the winter. Ahhhh. That's nice. Yes, sometimes I feel like Sasquatch when it comes to my carbon footprint, but being able to get into a warm vehicle on a cold day, priceless.

Just The Tips

The DIA Sky Bridge

If you travel a lot, learn the hacks for the airports you go through. I live in Denver so one example is the Sky Bridge. It's a great way to get in your steps and to skip the longer security lines.

Just The Tips

Take Pictures Of People So You Remember Them

If you're bad with names, take pictures. Taking a selfie with someone will not only help you remember who they are, but it will also help you remember the context in which you met. You'll have the date, time and location of when the picture was taken and that should be enough to commit them to memory for good.

Just The Tips

Add Pictures To Your CRM

Use the pictures on your phone, in Facebook, Instagram, LinkedIn, whatever and add them to the person's contact file in your CRM. If you're either bad with names or bad with faces, you'll know who they are every time your phone rings.

Just The Tips

Don't Leave Your Earpiece In The Sun

I don't think I had ever burned the inside of my ear before I made that mistake. Learn from my mistakes and do not leave your earbuds, headphones or Bluetooth earpiece sitting in the sun. Ouch.

Just The Tips

Set Up Google Alerts For Everything

Google alerts are an amazing tool. Set them up for you, your business, your industry, your kids, whatever. And every time there is something new on the internet about that subject, you'll get notified.

Just The Tips

October Is The Finest Month

For traveling in the northern hemisphere and certainly North America. If you like it further north, take a jacket. If you prefer the warmer climate to the south, pack your flip flops. Regardless, October seems to be the ideal time to travel North America, from a weather standpoint.

Just The Tips

Ease Up On The Hashtags

It's worse than your bedazzling. If you want to use a
ton of hashtags in your social media posts, then use
the key ones in your post, and the other hundred
you're still going to use should go in the comments.
That way, they still pop up on hashtag searches, and
your audience doesn't have to look at your gaudy
chandelier like posts.

Just The Tips

Social Media Platforms Are Search Engines

Think about it. You can search for anything and anyone on Facebook, Instagram, LinkedIn, etc. So treat them the way you would Google, as you can find things the same way you would there. If you're looking for an individual, the social media search engines are far superior to the innerwebs ones.

Make Real Connections

Your sales job is not some assembly line type of business. You work with real people, so make real connections. These are people just like you with parents and children and jobs and hobbies. So connect with people in a real way and you'll not only have better sales success, you'll have better relationships, to boot.

Help Your Colleagues Succeed

We've already talked about how you get more than you give, so take that to heart with your business. If you help your colleagues, even your "competitors" succeed, you will too. Help your colleagues solve problems. Give them ideas for things that are working for you. Be a leader in your business and your industry and it will come back to you in ways that make you even more successful.

Just The Tips

Learn The Difference Between Holidays

Memorial Day is when we remember American service members who died in the line of duty. Veterans Day is when we recognize those who served in military. And Armed Forces Day is the day for active duty members. Thank you all for your service.

Death And Divorce Are Good For Business

This is a horrible fact of life and certainly of sales life. People die. People get divorced. It happens. A lot. But a good salesperson comes from a place of wanting to help people and these are times in peoples' lives when they need real help. If you focus on that, deriving business from death and divorce won't seem so morbid.

Just The Tips

Your Competitors Should Be Contacts

If you have really great competition, they likely have an abundance mentality, as should you. You, and they, should be willing to share what makes you, or them, successful if that's the case. Your competitors might just be some of your greatest advocates if you all share the same mindset.

Just The Tips

Your Colleagues Should Be Contacts

Your colleagues should be your greatest cheerleaders. If not, you might want to examine your work life a little closer. But seriously, my team knows to get my name out when there are conversations going on about real estate and mortgages. And more importantly, the ones that are no longer on my team do too. As long as they get the same TOM reminders that I am still in the business, of course.

Two Sides To Every Story

Try to remember when listening to a controversial tale or subject, whether it be gossip, work related or otherwise, that odds are you are hearing one side of the story. There is another side of that story out there and the truth is likely in the middle.

Just The Tips

Gatekeepers Go Home At 5:00

If your sales gig includes some telemarketing, then you know what the gatekeeper is and what they do. But the gatekeeper is a 9 to 5 gig, I assure you. So, if you're fried on not being able to get past the gatekeepers to the decision makers, try calling after 5. Decision makers don't split at 5 and you might have some luck in getting through to them.

Use A Clients' Phone To Call Their Competitor

If you're selling a product like say, pharmaceuticals, where you sell the same product to multiple people or places, try doing your cold calling from one of your customer's phones. If a doctor's office sees another doctor's office on the caller ID, they are more likely to answer it then if it's a cell phone for a sales rep.

Just The Tips

The Armrest On The Aisle Goes Up

Yeah, that one. Oh, you thought only the ones in-between the seats went up? Nope. That one does, too. There's a button under the armrest on most of them. Just fidget with it and you'll figure it out. But it does have to be down for take-off and landing.

The Dog Park

This is one of the single greatest networking venues on the planet. And you already have something in common with everyone there. And the dogs do the introductions for you. It doesn't get any better than that for networking.

Check Your Spare Tire

I like to help stranded motorists. I stop almost every time I see someone in need of some assistance on the road. But, I cannot believe how many of them are flat tires and they either don't have a spare tire, or their spare tire is flat. A spare tire has been a basic insurance policy of sorts since the dawn of the automobile so make sure you have one and that it can actually be used when needed.

Just The Tips

Remind People What You Do All The Time

In sales there are only two things you need to get across. Who you are and what you do. Make sure everyone knows that you sell real estate. Or cars. Or mortgages. Or widgets. Or whatever. You wouldn't believe how many times I come across someone who says they didn't know that so-and-so was a real estate agent. How did they not know that? Because the real estate agent failed in making sure they knew.

Do Whip Posts

This means you need to post things in social media that are strictly for the purposes of generating likes and comments. Typically, asking for opinions on certain subjects is common. The idea isn't to have some kind of poll as to see who prefers Burger King to McDonalds but rather to get people looking at your social media assets. Who you are and what you do, right?

Just The Tips

Rock Jocks Provide Great Whip Fodder

Radio DJs have a lot of air time to fill between songs, especially during the morning and evening hours. Every radio station has some kind of morning and drive time show. Well, those guys have to find content that's interesting to their audience, just like you, so pay attention to what they're talking about as it will likely spark ideas for your own social media, videos, podcasts, whatever.

Don't Be Shy

This is the curse of a salesperson. You cannot be shy. You cannot be an introvert. Sales is about being outgoing and friendly. Meeting new people. Building relationships. Making friends and eventually clients. If you are in sales, or want to be, you have got to get over your shyness.

Size Matters

No, not that. I mean the size of your database. You need a robust database to do any good marketing or prospecting and the more the merrier. He who has the most friends wins.

HARO

Check this one out. It stands for Help A Reporter Out and it is a great way to contribute to articles and stories on subjects you're an expert on without having to draft entire articles or books. Being published, on any level, is great for both exposure and credibility, and this happens to be an easy way to do it.

Just The Tips

Watch What You Eat Before A Travel Day

Do you particularly like airport bathrooms? Lots of good privacy there, right? Or those big spacious ones on airplanes? Always good for a long…rest. Well, obviously none of us do so don't go to town on the mango habanero hot wings the night before you have to travel. Trust me on this one.

Remember The Name

We all could be better at remembering people's names. So, after you meet someone, use their name, and remind them of your name the next time you see them, or even the next few times you see them. Or use some other name remembering tool and it will help both of you remember.

Use A Cell Phone Case And Screen Protector

This is the very best and very cheapest insurance in the whole wide world that you can buy. A good cell phone case and a good screen protector are a hell of a lot cheaper than a new cell phone. Believe me, I know. I am that guy who will put his phone in his lap, right before getting out of the car, drop it on to the ground getting out of the car, and the proceed to accidentally kick it under the car. Yes, I've done that. More than once.

Just The Tips

Local Media People Make Great Contacts

Local media personalities know a ton of local people, have influence with a ton of local people, and are at the top of their game when it comes to social interaction, video and audio work, and marketing. These are good people to know for a thousand reasons.

Wedding Ring Reminder

I know this sounds a little silly but it works. If I need a short term reminder and I can't use my cell phone to send myself a note, like when I am driving, I will put my wedding ring on another finger and use it as a reminder. Kind of like the old piece of string trick. It feels awkward and serves as a great reminder to do something before putting it back on my ring finger.

Stay Current In Your Social Media

I am always stunned by people doing things on social media that were likely a good way to build an audience and get traction two years ago but don't apply today. I even see people teaching antiquated methods of how to use social media that would actually do more harm than good. Make sure you know what Facebook, Instagram, Snapchat, etc. are up do when it comes to their algorithms and business practices.

Just The Tips

People Read Reviews For Everything

I never really cared what other people posted in the way of reviews on different products and services but now I even find myself looking. My wife will read a thousand reviews on a product and I think I once bought a car because the TV ad had the same kind of dog as me. Believe me, people are looking at that stuff when it comes to you, your business, your service and your product.

Just The Tips

Use The Social Media Your Clients Use

If your ideal client is 65 years old, don't prospect or advertise on Snapchat. If your ideal client is 25 years old, don't bother with Facebook. It's important to know what your ideal client/customer is up to so that you can identify how to reach out to them better.

Just The Tips

Use Funny Pictures For Boring Posts

Not that I would ever recommend boring posts but sometimes you just have to get some information out there that isn't exactly the pinnacle of entertainment. Try using a funny photo with your boring post as it will get more engagement as well as get better results in social media algorithms.

Just The Tips

Neighborhood Facts Are Fun Posts

You've got to be active in your community and neighborhood, including social media, so make sure you are giving good information about the neighborhood and community to the neighborhood and community. This is a great way to establish yourself as that neighborhood and community expert.

Just The Tips

Silly Holidays Make For Fun Posts

There are at least a couple of bizarre and obscure holidays every day of the year. Find out what they are and use them to your advantage. We use them to come up with silly contests and give away cool prizes in order to get better social media traction and edge ranking.

Post Real Things About You

When you post on social media, and you'd better be, the majority of your posts should be personal, not business. At least 50/50, anyway. And when you're posting personal things, be really real. Your clients and customers are human and they want to know that you are, too. They have the same highs and lows. The same successes and failures. The good, the bad and the ugly. So, be a person on social media and not a sales machine.

Just The Tips

Use Your Actual Photo In Your Web Assets.

If you're a professional, a picture of a kitten or a cartoon or a flower is not an okay substitute for a picture of you. I won't even accept a social media request from someone I can't see. And again, make sure it's the same picture across all your web assets to further that branding and recognition.

Just The Tips

Shower Radio

Whenever someone asks me what the very best thing I ever bought for less than 50 bucks is…you got it, my shower radio. Cheap, easy to use, waterproof, Bluetooth, terrestrial radio, etc. I get some weather and news in the morning, maybe a little music, and I have to stand there anyway, so I may as well get more out of that time.

Just The Tips

Traveling With Cologne And Perfume

If you travel with your favorite fragrance, overdo it when you're actually traveling. I find that going insane with my Aqua Velva will sometimes get me an empty row on an airplane or an empty seat next to me on the train.

Just The Tips

If You Only Have 5 Star Reviews, We All Know Its BS

You can't please all the people all the time, right? Well, having the occasional bad review only proves you're human. If you only have perfect reviews, people all know those reviews came from your Mom and Aunt Gertie. But make sure you know how to properly respond to those reviews, too.

Respond To Bad Reviews

If you can, you should respond to all reviews, but make sure you respond to the bad ones. Ignoring the negative reviews is a mistake. Apologize and even briefly explain what occurred but do not be defensive or attack the person reviewing you. That review is no longer important when it comes to that client or customer but it is very important to the future ones.

Set A Timer For The Time Sucks

So, you like to waste time surfing Facebook? Me, too! Ever heard of The Chive? Oof. So limit that time, that screen time, like we would with our kids, and set reminders and timers so you don't waste the whole day doing it. You want to play on social media for an hour? Great. Then set a timer for one hour and when it goes off, get back to work.

Just The Tips

Have Fun With Telemarketers

Telemarketers are sales people, too. And they are regular people, too. You might be missing out on a client, a friend or just a great conversation with another like-minded individual so turn those telemarketing calls into real conversations.

Make Sure Your S.O. Is On Your Team

My wife, my amazing wife, is also a member of my team. She is always combing social media for opportunities to recommend me, constantly referring her friends and family and knows how to prospect for me. Make sure your significant other is in the game with you and helping you with your lead generation.

Just The Tips

Always Put Your Audience First

In everything you do in your marketing and prospecting; always consider the audience first. Is this valuable to them? Is it something they want to see or hear or watch? Is it for the greater good and not self-serving? If you put them first, they will recognize it, buy from you and refer other people you can put first who will then buy from you, too.

Just The Tips

Your Ideal Audience

Even better, fine-tune your content for your ideal audience. Is your content something that is not just going to attract customers or clients, but is it going to attract the ones that can work with you and that you want to work with?

Sell With Story Telling

Stories are a great way to make real connections with people. People want to know that you're a real person, just like they are, and sharing stories is a great way to do that. You're going to have things in common with everyone you meet and sharing stories is a great way to find out what those things are.

Just The Tips

A Smart Watch Saves The Cell Phone Battery

I know not everyone is into watches. And I know not everyone is into consumer tech gear. But, having an iWatch or a Gear will enable you to see what is on your phone without having to pull it out of your pocket every time it vibrates. This will extend the life of the cell phone battery and we've all been at that point where it's either find an outlet or die.

Just The Tips

Places You Hate Are Full Of Leads

The dentist. The doctor. The accountant. Nobody likes to go to these places but if you go with your prospecting and marketing hat on, as you should everywhere you go, you'll see that the dentist, the doctor, the nurses, the hygienists, the accountant, the patients and other people getting taxes done are all potential clients and customers.

People Living In Your Head Rent Free

This one has always been a big deal to me and while I am going to preach to you about it, I'm not 100% good at it. People are going to do things you don't like. They are going to do things to you that you don't like. They are going to do things to other people that you don't like. But they've already done it. It's over. It's in the past. Let it go. Stop thinking about the people that behaved poorly and move on.

Have a Niche

I don't care what it is, just do something unique. Maybe it's your product. Maybe it's your branding. Maybe it's your clientele. Whatever it is, have a niche that distinguishes and separates you from the competition. I'm pretty sure you're not the only person selling what you're selling.

Just The Tips

Cope With Failure

Sales people have to be able to do this. You have to be able to accept failure, get back up, learn from it, and continue to grow and develop. Show me a sales person who hasn't experienced failure and I will show you someone who's probably a sales manager. Seriously, find your best methods for getting past failure and making sure you learn from those failures.

Know How To Manage Inconsistent Income

This is a pretty big deal with salespeople, although it's mostly your fault. You know when you get busy with actual business, you forget to spend time finding more business. It happens to all of us. But that income roller coaster is the result and you need to learn to manage that. Set up your own LLC and pay yourself regular amounts. Or have a savings account of sorts that helps you manage those ups and downs. Just find a way to balance the inconsistent income.

Just The Tips

Manage Expectations

It is always best to be up front and straight forward
from the beginning of your sales cycle. Give
everyone realistic expectations on costs, on timelines,
on everything they should expect through the course
of doing business with you.

Just The Tips

Time Your Internet Leads

I never recommend buying leads or using internet leads, but every buyer and every salesperson is different. If you are utilizing internet leads, make sure you can track what time they were online as that is likely a good window to be able to reach them back.

Just The Tips

Don't Sell People, Help People

Whatever it is you're selling, people need it. They may not know they need it, or understand why they need it so it's your job to make that clear. Don't think of your job as a sales job, think of it as a helping job. Help people instead of selling them.

Have Good Content

Make sure all your "marketing" has good content. Content that is for the greater good of the audience. Don't do marketing that's all about you and your company and how great you are. Do marketing that is of value to your ideal client or customer.

Just The Tips

Who Is Watching Your Videos

If you're doing videos, and you should be, it doesn't matter whether they are live videos on Facebook, Instagram, IGTV or higher production videos. Consider who is going to watch them. And consider whether or not they would want to watch them. Videos about your business are likely boring. Videos about you are not.

Pets

I'm not saying you need to have pets, although they are great for companionship, relieving stress and always having someone who's glad to see you, but you gotta like animals. Someone once said they wouldn't trust someone their dog doesn't like. Well, I don't trust people who don't like animals. I'm not talking about someone who's allergic to cats, mind you, you just can't hate animals.

Body Language

Want to communicate better with your clients and customers in person? Pay attention to their body language, mimic what you can and make them more comfortable. Nonverbal communication is bigger and more influential than the words coming out of your mouth so do what you can to communicate as best you can and you'll make better connections.

Just The Tips

Attitude Is Important

It might be the most important thing. I think a positive attitude likely trumps a lot of other "skills" a salesperson needs to have. It's not always easy, but hanging out with positive people or doing hard work that benefits others are the kinds of things that can help breed a positive attitude.

Just The Tips

Rotate Your Tires

This is a great car maintenance and frugality tip. My daily driver has a full size spare so I get to do five tire rotations and because I do it regularly, I probably get twice the mileage out of the tires that I would normally get and certainly twice what the warranty is.

Be Yourself, Including Your Interests

I see so many people do their marketing and prospecting in such a boring and vanilla manner, mostly because they are afraid of offending someone or some group and missing out on that business. But the result is that they actually lose more business because they come off so vanilla and boring. Be yourself, attract people like you and don't worry about the rest.

Let People Vent

For the most part, the sales process, whether it's getting a mortgage, a new house, a new car or whatever, is likely a stressful process. Sometimes people just need to vent. So, let them. Don't exacerbate their stress by venting back, just listen. Venting is a great way to relieve stress and you can do that for your clients and customers. Let them vent.

Ask Questions That Make Them Think

Do this for a number of reasons. It makes people slow down and really consider their options with what they're buying. It gives you a great opportunity to be a good listener and figure out who people are and how to really help them. And it differentiates you from everyone else who asks the questions that get the old, knee jerk answers that we all give to simple questions.

You're Only As Good As Your Last Deal

We all know that's not really the case, but that is the perception, so you have to embrace it. You have to be on your game on every deal. The next referral depends on it. Having that client or customer as a repeat client and referral source depends on it. Having the continued relationship with the referral partner that sent them to you depends on it.

Work On Your Personal Relationships

This is so important for both your personal and business lives. Those personal relationships lead to business relationships which lead to more personal relationships and so on. This is a major piece of the repeat and referral business puzzle.

Just The Tips

Add Value For Your Business Partners

Refer them business. Help with their marketing.
Mastermind ideas with them. They want to do more
business, too. Help them do that.

Be The First Point Of Contact

Most sales, like home buying, require more than one sales person to be involved. If you're that first point of contact, you control the deal. You decide who to refer the client/customer to for the other pieces, like a real estate agent or mortgage broker. Being the first point of contact is both empowering and enables you to refer business out to your referral partners.

Just The Tips

Be Nice To Everyone

Everyone has personal issues. I do. You do. We all do. You never know if the customer service agent you're frustrated with lost her mother this week. Or if the server in that restaurant is getting evicted from his apartment. Or maybe your mortgage broker had to put down his dog. Whatever it is, try to remember that we all have crap we're going through and that we all need to be nice to one another.

Just The Tips

Always Be Prospecting

This leads to Always Be Closing. We all have a tendency to neglect our prospecting when we are busy with actual work. That will hurt you a month, or two, or three down the road. Even when you're super busy, make sure you are carving out time to prospect so that you're still busy in the months to come.

Just The Tips

Amazon. That is all.

Seriously. What a world we live in. I remember I need something. Amazon. I think of a gift I want to get for someone. Amazon. I need a new whatever. Amazon.

Just The Tips

Know Where Your Business Comes From

Is your business repeat clients? Is it client referrals?
Is it coming from referral partners? From advertising?
Leads? Do you know? Figure that out and do more
of what works.

Just The Tips

Time Management Is Key

A great colleague of mine once said "Happiness is a well-oiled calendar" and he is right. Good time management and good calendar management are key components to good work productivity and good life/work balance.

Just The Tips

Your Voice Mail Is Full

No, no and NO! Seriously, WTF is wrong with you?
You're in sales and your voice mail is full? I sure
hope it isn't a lead or prospect that was referred by
you very best past client that just got that message.
Do not let your voice mail get full. Not ever. Not even
once.

Just The Tips

Just Solve Problems

Sales can be pretty easy that way. If someone needs to buy what you're selling, there's a reason. They need or want it. They likely have some kind of "pain point" that can be solved to a degree with your product. So just solve problems. Fix those pain points.

Get Involved In Trade Organizations

Almost every sales industry has trade organizations that provide networking, education, camaraderie and the opportunity to make contacts, build your contact database, forge new relationships, make friends and eventually clients and customers.

Just The Tips

Your Job Is To Generate Leads

I ask people in sales what their job is all the time. Most are happy to give me their elevator speech or some corny version of what their job really isn't. For a real estate agent, for example, without generating leads you don't have contracts and inspections and closings and so on. Your job is to generate leads. The rest is a byproduct of that.

Just The Tips

Share What You Do Outside Of Work

A big part of sales is establishing solid interpersonal relationships. We all know the "know, like and trust" bit so sharing what you do in your "free" time is going to help you connect with other people who like to do the same things.

Just The Tips

Set The Precedent For Communication

If you are Johnny On The Spot with returning phone calls, then you have to keep doing that. If you take calls late at night, then keep doing that. Don't set a precedent with your communication only to fail at your own M.O. right after.

Bad Clients Refer Bad Clients

This is big if you want to have a repeat and referral business. We all know that people are the direct result of the people they spend the most time with. So remember that your pain in the ass clients are going to refer more pains in the ass.

Just The Tips

Chiropractors

I have to admit, I spent most of my life as a chiro-skeptic and even had a couple of bad experiences but if you find a good one, it's priceless. I started because of an injury but have gone back every month ever since, and especially when I am traveling. It just helps me stay loose, sleep better and work better especially when dealing with strange beds and airplane seats.

Just The Tips

Big Companies Have Lots Of Employees

Pay attention to where your clients and customers work. If it's a big company like Apple or Amazon or Microsoft, they have a ton of coworkers to refer to you. Having happy clients and customers at a company like that could be a goldmine of referrals.

Just The Tips

Use Your Actual Picture

Don't use a picture of your cat in social media profile. Don't use your 1985 headshot on your real estate yard signs. A big part of sales is letting people know who you are and not using real and current pictures doesn't accomplish that.

Be The Trusted Authority

Know the difference between being a trusted advisor and being a trusted authority and strive for the latter. An advisor makes recommendations people either accept or don't. An authority makes recommendations that people exercise unequivocally.

Just The Tips

Fake It Till You Make It

There's some solid truth to this old saying.
Sometimes you have to fake it until you make it.
People don't want to work with someone who doesn't
know what they're doing and when you're new, you
don't know what the hell you're doing. It's just a fact.

9 Volt Batteries

I love this one. These things are virtually extinct except for a few really important things, namely smoke detectors. Lifesaving smoke detectors. So if you want a great, easy, cheap gift. Send people 9 volt batteries for their smoke detectors. It is huge on the convenience scale and it shows you really care about people.

Millennial Employees

Here is a group of people that is well educated, highly motivated to earn money to pay off enormous student loan debt, and hasn't been poisoned by the working world yet. If you're hiring in sales, this group might very well be an ideal target for you.

Be Like Starbucks

This is the epitome of the customer experience. It's the same latte every time. It's the same process every time. It's the same expectation every time. And they keep coming back. Not to mention pretty cool tech and decent coffee. Even if you only had cool tech and decent coffee you'd be winning.

Just The Tips

Conference With Like Minded People

If you're going to go to conferences, and you'd better be, make sure the other attendees do things the way you do and think the way you think. While good conference content should be rule number one, the attendees you get to network with and share ideas with and strategize with should be a close second.

Just The Tips

Embrace Technology

Yes, change is difficult. Yes, technology has a learning curve. But, just like Quicken is to mortgage originators, Zillow is to real estate agents and Carvana is to car sales people, the technology is going to win. So you'd better get on board because the technology is not going anywhere.

Just The Tips

Dirty Diapers At The Beach

Wrap your belongings in a diaper when you want to trot off the beach and into the water. Nobody is going to mess with what looks like a used diaper while you're not watching.

Don't Fight For Overhead Space

Either check your bags, or if you have to carry on, pay to book the seat on the bulkhead. There's no seat in front of you to put things under, so they have to let you use the overhead space at no additional charge.

Get Back To Work

Most sales people have some sort of attention deficit, especially me. How much time do I waste on Facebook every day? I don't know but it's a lot. So, I actually have a giant sign in my office reminding me to get back to work.

Just The Tips

Get Reviews

If your product is something more significant than a lightbulb, people are going to check you out before buying. Make sure that your past clients, customers and colleagues are writing reviews about you and their experiences. Zillow, Facebook, Yelp, Google and LinkedIn, to name a few, all have great resources for those reviews.

Just The Tips

Get People To Read Your Reviews

If your potential clients and customers haven't already done so, steer them towards the places where other people have written reviews about you, your services or your products. This is a big deal with monster operations like Amazon and EBay so it should be important to you, too.

Consider Your Competition When Hiring

When you are choosing an assistant, or a transaction coordinator or any one on your team ask yourself if you would want this person working for your competition. If the answer is no, you should probably hire them.

Post Your Successes

People want to work with people that are busy and successful so let them know that you are. Post your closings, your big sales, your great successes and let people know that you are busy and successful.

Just The Tips

Third Party Postings

You know those group post inquiries about the best real estate agent? The best mortgage lender? The best car dealer? Well, typically the one with the most recommendations wins so if you see those posts, alert your friends to go say something nice about you in the comments.

Just The Tips

End Of Year Campaigns

I don't care how you do it. Text, Sly Broadcast, email, mail, the phone, whatever. Make a great script and reach out to everyone you worked with over the course of the year and thank them for working with you.

Just The Tips

One Thing At A Time

There is so much noise out there for lead generation ideas, marketing tactics, prospecting programs and so on that it's hard to tune it all out. Pick one that you think will work for you. Implement it. Manipulate to meet your style. Automate and systemize it. Then go choose and work another.

Airlines Partner With Cell Providers

Did you know some airlines have partnership with wireless carriers? Find out which one has a partnership with your carrier and odds are good that your on-board WiFi will be free. If you travel a lot, that adds up flight after flight, even if it isn't always the cheapest flight.

Just The Tips

Have Good Mobile Tech

Make sure the apps you're using are on your phone, your tablet, your computer, everything. Not that working on your phone is ideal, but you want to be able to do it if necessary. Having operating systems and applications that all talk to each other no matter which device is critical to good tech use.

Future Casting

Future casting is one of the greatest sales tricks in the book. Well, maybe not in this book, but in a lot of sales books. You have to get your client or customer to see themselves driving that car. Living in that house. Making money on that investment. If you can future cast them into it, they'll buy it.

Just The Tips

Email Is Not Life Or Death

Nobody expects you to reply to email instantly. Nobody even expects you to treat it like a text or DM. Don't let email derail your work. Email is a distracting demon that becomes less and less important with every passing day so don't let it run you.

Do Not Be Google

One of the greatest time sucks I've ever had is being Google. Answering questions my team should be answering. Or a real estate agent should be answering. Or an insurance agent. Or a number of other sources, even the internet. Do not be Google. Condition your clients and customers and colleagues to get the answers they need from where they should be getting them.

The Doctor Doesn't Do The Billing

He has someone to do that. And to check in his patients. And to give them paper gowns. And to show them to the examination room. He doesn't do everything in his practice. He does the things he likes and the things that make him money. And so should you.

Just The Tips

Multi-Tasking Is A Myth

You really can't do two important things at the same time and do them well. Yes, yes I know. You're a rock star at multi-tasking. No, you're not. You rock at going to the bathroom and playing on your cell phone at the same time. When it's something important, eliminate the distractions, focus on one thing, do it fast and do it well. Then move onto another.

Just The Tips

Your Only Competition Is You

You don't have to be better than the other guy. You just have to be better today than you were yesterday and better tomorrow than you are today.

Just The Tips

Buy Flowers

For no reason at all. Your significant other, your mother, your daughter, your employees, your colleagues, whomever. Just make the gesture to let them know you were thinking about them.

Just The Tips

Buy Dinner

Out with a colleague? Maybe you're on a date? Just pick up the check. That kind of thing, that generosity, will come back to you tenfold in the future in ways you can't imagine.

Serenity Prayer

I don't know the exact prayer, mind you, but I know the essence of it and it is legit. Way legit. Let go of the things you can't control, roll with the punches on things you do have to deal with, and learn the difference. This is life changing in my mind. Do not stress out about the things that are going to happen or haven't even happened yet. That is not going to make those situations any better.

Just The Tips

Don't Be A Packrat

Live light. Only keep what you need. Trust me on this one and learn from my mistakes. I recently moved from a home my wife and three children lived in for 16 years. You have no idea how much crap you can accumulate in 16 years. If you haven't used something in a few years, get rid of it. On the off chance you need it again, buy another one.

Just The Tips

Life Is About How You React

A group of 12 year olds showed me some enlightening stuff years ago. They were competing in what we used to call Olympics of the Mind building a balsa wood structure that had to bear weight. The most weight wins. And they did. All the way to the state tournament. It was there they realized they had built the latest one differently. Then and there they decided to make the best alterations they could, hope for the best, and be ready to compete again the next year. Life isn't about how you act. It's about how you react. How do you roll with the punches?

Play Chess

If you don't know how to play, learn. If you know how, play once in a while. Chess is a great game to focus on strategy, to use your ability to think ahead, and it can be a great way to do something mentally productive at a casual pace.

Just The Tips

Twenty Dollar Lending Rule

If someone asks to borrow twenty bucks, give it to them. If they don't pay it back, you just bought someone who behaves like that out of your life for a very cheap price. They'll avoid you forever and they will never ask to borrow money again.

Just The Tips

Take Pictures

Take pictures of everything and everywhere. It's so easy to do now with everyone carrying a camera everywhere they go and it's so easy to keep and store them, so you'll have them forever.

Anything Times Zero Is Still Zero

This is like a counting your chickens before they hatch thing. I wish I had a dollar for every time someone told me about the deals they are going to close. Not the ones they have closed. This is a common theme among sales people so remember; anything times zero is still zero.

Let Them Do It At 80%

One of the biggest issues I see with sales people hiring an assistant is that they truly believe nobody can do the tasks better than they can. Well, can they do it 80% as well as you can? Then let them. Spend that time doing things that you like or really make you money. Or both.

Just The Tips

You Have To Sell Your Referral Partners

If you want to have really great referral partner relationships you have to do this. When I am referring a client to a real estate agent, I make sure that client knows this person is the very best real estate agent that ever lived and they would be fools to use one of the lesser one million agents out there.

Just The Tips

Fine Tune Your Audience

As time goes on, you need to be fine tuning your audience. On social media you can unfriend people that aren't in your perfect audience so you can add others. In your contact database, you can remove old contacts and get more time to contact the ones you do want. Eventually your entire audience will only be your ideal clients and customers.

Just The Tips

Set Manageable Goals

We all know how important goal setting is but you have to be smart about what the goals are. I see sales people set the bar very, very low and have zero motivation to do any better and I see people set the bar so high that disappointment is a certainty. When setting your goals, be very astute so as not to shoot too low or too high.

Just The Tips

Grammarly

I think we all know the importance of good speech and good writing so double and triple check the words coming out of your mouth and your computer. I actually heard a sales person recently say how they do speaking very good. No, you don't.

Just The Tips

Every Call Is The First Call

If you treat every phone call like it's the very first call with that lead, customer, client or advocate, you'll stay more engaged and have more productive results from your phone conversations.

Just The Tips

Long Presentations Have Shorter Results

I catch myself getting long winded in classes and presentations all the time and I know when I do, the audience isn't as interested, the impact isn't as great, the conversion isn't as high and the sales process suffers.

Believe In Your Product.

If you're not enamored with what you sell, don't. If it isn't something you wouldn't buy, you're not going to succeed in selling it. Maybe you need to change products. Maybe you need to change companies. Maybe you need to change careers but if you can't sell you, you can't sell anyone else.

Just The Tips

Tie A Yellow Ribbon

It doesn't have to be yellow, or a ribbon, but tie something to the handle of your suitcase, because it looks like every other suitcase on the carousel. This will make it easier and faster for you to get your bag and get out of the airport.

Just The Tips

Ask Questions

A lot of sales is answering a lot of questions. So ask pointed questions to really make your customers and clients think and it will show you're genuinely interested in them and their answers, as well.